The Complete Australian Cookbook

Quick Easy and Delicious Traditional Australian Dishes

BY: JUSTICE CORONZIA

TABLE OF CONTENTS

RECIPES

1.Aussie Meat Pie

Prep Time: 30 mins
Cook Time: 45 mins
Total Time: 1 hr 15 mins
Servings: 6

Ingredients:

- 1 lb ground beef
- 1 onion, lightly chop-up
- 2 cloves garlic, chop-up
- 2 tbsp tomato paste
- 1 cup of beef broth
- 1 tbsp Worcestershire sauce
- 1 tbsp all-purpose flour
- Salt and pepper as needed
- 2 sheets puff pastry
- 1 egg, beaten (for egg wash)

Instructions:

1. Preheat the oven to 190°C (375°F).
2. Brown the ground beef in a pan over medium heat.
3. Add chop-up garlic and diced onion. Simmer the onion up to it becomes transparent.
4. Add flour, Worcestershire sauce, beef broth, and tomato paste and stir. Once the mixture thickens, simmer it.
5. As needed, add salt and pepper for seasoning.
6. Place one layer of puff pastry inside a pie plate.
7. Fill the pie plate with the meat mixture.
8. Seal the edges and cover with the second piece of puff pastry.
9. Apply beaten egg to the top.
10. Bake the pastry for 30 to 35 mins, or up to golden brown.

Nutrition:

Cals: 400 per serving, Protein: 20g, Carbs: 25g
Fat: 25g, Fiber: 2g

2.Vegemite Toast with Avocado

Prep Time: 5 mins
Total Time: 5 mins
Servings: 2

Ingredients:

- 2 slices whole grain bread, toasted
- Butter (non-compulsory)
- Vegemite

- 1 avocado, split
- Red pepper flakes (non-compulsory)

Instructions:

1. If you want, you can butter the toasted bread.
2. On top of the buttery bread, spread a thin coating of Vegemite.
3. Top with split avocado.
4. Sprinkle with red pepper flakes if desired.

Nutrition:

Cals: 200 per serving, Protein: 4g, Carbs: 20g, Fat: 12g, Fiber: 5g

3.Kangaroo Kebabs with Bush Tomato Chutney

Prep Time: 20 mins
Cook Time: 10 mins
Total Time: 30 mins
Servings: 4

Ingredients:

- 1 lb kangaroo meat, slice into cubes
- 2 tbsp olive oil
- 1 tsp ground cumin
- 1 tsp ground coriander
- Salt and pepper as needed
- Wooden skewers, soaked in water
- Bush tomato chutney for serving

Instructions:

1. Mix kangaroo cubes, olive oil, salt, pepper, ground cumin, and ground coriander in a bowl. For at least fifteen mins, marinate.
2. Skewers dipped in water are threaded with marinated kangaroo cubes.
3. The kebabs Must be cooked to your preference after around 5 mins on every side of the grill.
4. Present alongside a side dish of bush tomato chutney.

Nutrition:

Cals: 200 per serving, Protein: 25g, Carbs: 2g
Fat: 10g, Fiber: 1g

4.Barramundi with Macadamia Pesto

Prep Time: 15 mins
Cook Time: 15 mins
Total Time: 30 mins
Servings: 4

Ingredients:

- 4 barramundi fillets
- 1 cup of fresh basil leaves
- 1/2 cup of macadamia nuts

- 1/2 cup of Parmesan cheese that has been finely grated
- 2 cloves garlic, chop-up
- 1/2 cup of olive oil
- Salt and pepper as needed
- Lemon wedges for serving

Instructions:

1. Set oven temperature to 400°F, or 200°C.
2. Rub some salt and pepper on the barramundi fillets.
3. Add the basil, macadamia nuts, Parmesan cheese, and chop-up garlic to a mixer. Pulse up to chop-up lightly.
4. Olive oil Must be added gradually while the mixer is operating to achieve a pesto-like consistency.
5. Arrange the barramundi fillets onto a baking sheet and generously cover with macadamia pesto.
6. Bake the fish for 12 to 15 mins, or up to it is thoroughly done.
7. Accompany with wedges of lemon.

Nutrition:

Cals: 350 per serving, Protein: 30g, Carbs: 2g
Fat: 25g, Fiber: 1g

5.Pavlova with Fresh Berries

Prep Time: 20 mins
Cook Time: 1 hr
Total Time: 1 hr 20 mins
Servings: 8

Ingredients:

- 4 Big egg whites
- 1 cup of granulated sugar
- 1 tsp white vinegar
- 1 tsp vanilla extract
- 1 tbsp cornstarch
- 1 cup of whipped cream
- Fresh berries (strawberries, blueberries, raspberries)

Instructions:

1. Set oven temperature to 300°F, or 150°C.
2. Beat the egg whites up to stiff peaks form in a clean, dry basin.
3. Add the sugar progressively while beating the mixture up to it becomes glossy.
4. Stir in the cornflour, vinegar, and vanilla essence. Toss gently to mix.
5. Form the meringue into a circle and place it on a baking pan lined with parchment paper.
6. Bake the pavlova for one hr, or up to the outside is crisp.

7. Let it cool down fully.
8. Before serving, decorate with fresh berries and whipped cream.

Nutrition:

Cals: 250 per serving, Protein: 2g, Carbs: 50g, Fat: 5g, Fiber: 2g

6.Australian Lamb Roast

Prep Time: 15 mins
Cook Time: 1 hr 30 mins
Total Time: 1 hr 45 mins
Servings: 6

Ingredients:

- 1 leg of lamb
- 4 cloves garlic, split
- Rosemary sprigs
- 2 tbsp olive oil
- Salt and pepper as needed
- 1 cup of red wine (for basting)
- 1 cup of beef or lamb broth

Instructions:

1. Preheat the oven to 190°C (375°F).
2. Slices of garlic and sprigs of rosemary Must be inserted into the lamb through tiny incisions.
3. Season the lamb with salt and pepper after rubbing it with olive oil.
4. The lamb Must be put in a roasting pan with a roasting rack.
5. Fill the pan's bottom with the red wine and broth.
6. Roast for one hr and thirty mins, or up to the internal temperature is at the doneness you choose.
7. Every thirty mins, baste the lamb with the pan juices.
8. Give the lamb some time to rest before slicing.

Nutrition:

Cals: 400 per serving, Protein: 30g, Carbs: 1g
Fat: 30g, Fiber: 0g

7.Lamington Pancakes

Prep Time: 15 mins
Cook Time: 15 mins
Total Time: 30 mins
Servings: 4

Ingredients:

- 1 cup of all-purpose flour
- 2 tbsp sugar
- 1 tsp baking powder
- 1/2 tsp baking soda

- 1/4 tsp salt
- 1 cup of buttermilk
- 1 Big egg
- 2 tbsp unsalted butter, dilute
- 1 tsp vanilla extract
- Shredded coconut for coating
- Chocolate sauce for drizzling
- Whipped cream and strawberries for serving

Instructions:

1. Mix the flour, sugar, baking soda, baking powder, and salt in a bowl.
2. Beat the egg, dilute butter, vanilla extract, and buttermilk together in a separate basin.
3. Mixing up to just combined, pour the wet components into the dry ingredients.
4. Over medium heat, preheat a nonstick skillet or griddle.
5. Spoon pancake mixture onto the griddle and heat it up to bubbles appear on top. Cook till golden brown after flipping.
6. While still warm, cover every pancake with shredded coconut.
7. Pour chocolate sauce over it.
8. Serve with strawberries and whipped cream.

Nutrition:

Cals: 300 per serving, Protein: 6g, Carbs: 40g
Fat: 12g, Fiber: 2g

8.Veggie-packed Aussie Burger

Prep Time: 20 mins
Cook Time: 15 mins
Total Time: 35 mins
Servings: 4

Ingredients:

- 1 lb ground beef or kangaroo
- 1/2 cup of breadcrumbs
- 1 egg
- 1 tsp Worcestershire sauce
- Salt and pepper as needed
- 4 whole grain burger buns
- Lettuce leaves
- Tomato slices
- Beetroot slices
- Pineapple rings
- Red onion rings
- Sauce of choice (ketchup, mayo, or barbecue sauce)

Instructions:

1. Mix the ground beef or kangaroo, egg, breadcrumbs, Worcestershire sauce, salt, and pepper in a bowl.

2. Separate the blend into four portions and form them into patties.
3. Cook the patties on a skillet or grill up to done to your preference.
4. Get the burger buns toasty.
5. Mix the lettuce, tomato, beetroot, pineapple, red onion, and sauce of your choice with the burgers.

Nutrition:

Cals: 450 per serving, Protein: 25g, Carbs: 35g
Fat: 20g, Fiber: 5g

9.Anzac Biscuits

Prep Time: 15 mins
Cook Time: 12 mins
Total Time: 27 mins
Servings: 24

Ingredients:

- 1 cup of rolled oats
- 1 cup of all-purpose flour
- 1 cup of shredded coconut
- 1 cup of brown sugar
- 1/2 cup of unsalted butter
- 2 tbsp golden syrup or honey
- 1 tsp baking soda
- 2 tbsp boiling water

Instructions:

1. Set oven temperature to 350°F (180°C) and place parchment paper on baking sheets.
2. Brown sugar, shredded coconut, flour, and rolled oats Must all be mixd in a big bowl.
3. Melt butter and golden syrup in a saucepan over low heat.
4. stir the baking soda with boiling water in a mini basin and stir it into the butter mixture.
5. Mixing up to well blended, pour the wet components into the dry ingredients.
6. Leaving room between every drop of the mixture, place spoonfuls onto the baking sheets that have been prepared.
7. Bake for ten to twelve mins, or up to well-browned.
8. Before moving the Anzac cookies to a wire rack, let them cool on the baking sheets.

Nutrition:

Cals: 150 per serving, Protein: 2g, Carbs: 20g
Fat: 7g, Fiber: 1g

10.Grilled Crocodile Skewers

Prep Time: 20 mins
Marination Time: 1 hr

Cook Time: 10 mins
Total Time: 1 hr 30 mins
Servings: 4

Ingredients:
- 1 lb crocodile meat, slice into skewer-friendly pieces
- 2 tbsp olive oil
- 2 cloves garlic, chop-up
- 1 tbsp lemon juice
- 1 tsp dried thyme
- Salt and pepper as needed
- Lemon wedges for serving

Instructions:
1. To make the marinade, mix olive oil, chop-up garlic, lemon juice, dried thyme, salt, and pepper in a bowl.
2. For at least an hr, marinate the crocodile meat in the marinade.
3. Set the grill's temperature to medium-high.
4. Put slices of marinated crocodile onto skewers.
5. Up to cooked through, grill skewers for 5 to 7 mins on every side.
6. Accompany with wedges of lemon.
7. Savour the grilled skewers of crocodile!

Nutrition (per serving):
Cals: 200, Protein: 25g, Carbs: 1g
Fat: 10g, Fiber: 0g

11.Wattleseed Damper Bread

Prep Time: 15 mins
Cook Time: 30 mins
Total Time: 45 mins
Servings: 6

Ingredients:
- 3 cups of self-rising flour
- 1/2 cup of wattleseed (roasted and ground)
- 1 tsp salt
- 1 cup of milk
- 1/2 cup of water
- Butter for serving

Instructions:
1. Preheat the oven to 190°C (375°F).
2. Mix wattleseed, salt, and self-rising flour in a bowl.
3. Mix in water and milk to make a soft dough.
4. Utilising a floured surface, knead the dough.
5. Create a circular loaf out of the dough.
6. Scratch the top of the loaf and place it on a baking pan.
7. Bake for 25 to 30 mins, or up to a tapped damper produces a hollow sound.

8. Accompany with butter.
9. Savour your damper bread with wattleseed!

Nutrition (per serving):
Cals: 250, Protein: 7g, Carbs: 50g, Fat: 1g, Fiber: 3g

12.Sydney Rock Oysters Kilpatrick

Prep Time: 10 mins
Cook Time: 10 mins
Total Time: 20 mins
Servings: 4

Ingredients:
- 12 Sydney rock oysters, shucked
- 6 slices bacon, cooked and cut up
- 1/4 cup of Worcestershire sauce
- 1 tbsp tomato ketchup
- 1 tbsp lemon juice
- Salt and pepper as needed
- Lemon wedges for serving

Instructions:
1. Set the oven to grill temperature.
2. Scoop the oysters and put them on a baking sheet.
3. Cut up bacon, Worcestershire sauce, tomato ketchup, lemon juice, salt, and pepper Must all be mixd in a bowl.
4. Dollop the concoction onto every oyster.
5. After 5 to 7 mins, or when the edges are bubbling, broil.
6. Accompany with wedges of lemon.
7. Kilpatrick, enjoy your Sydney rock oysters!

Nutrition (per serving):
Cals: 150, Protein: 12g, Carbs: 5g
Fat: 8g, Fiber: 0g

13.Kangaroo Steak with Red Wine Jus

Prep Time: 15 mins
Marination Time: 2 hrs
Cook Time: 10 mins
Total Time: 2 hrs 25 mins
Servings: 4

Ingredients:
- 4 kangaroo steaks
- 1/2 cup of red wine
- 2 tbsp olive oil
- 2 cloves garlic, chop-up
- 1 tsp dried rosemary
- Salt and pepper as needed

1. Mix red wine, olive oil, dried rosemary, chop-up garlic, salt, and pepper in a bowl.
2. Give the kangaroo steaks at least two hrs to marinate in the marinade.
3. Heat the pan or grill to a medium-high temperature.
4. Once the steaks are cooked to your preference, grill them for 4–5 mins on every side.
5. Before serving, let the steaks a few mins to rest.
6. With a red wine jus, serve.
7. Savour your red wine jus and kangaroo steak!

Nutrition (per serving):

Cals: 300, Protein: 25g, Carbs: 2g, Fat: 18g

Fiber: 0g

14. Tim Tam Milkshake

Prep Time: 5 mins
Total Time: 5 mins
Servings: 2

Ingredients:

- 4 Tim Tam cookies, crushed
- 2 cups of vanilla ice cream
- 1 cup of milk
- Whipped cream for topping
- Chocolate shavings for garnish

Instructions:

1. Blend together milk, vanilla ice cream, and crushed Tim Tam cookies in a blender.
2. Process till smooth.
3. Transfer to glasses.
4. Add chocolate shavings and whipped cream over top.
5. Savour your milkshake with Tim Tams!

Nutrition (per serving):

Cals: 500, Protein: 8g, Carbs: 60g, Fat: 25g

Fiber: 1g

15. Kangaroo Sausage Rolls

Prep Time: 15 mins
Cook Time: 25 mins
Total Time: 40 mins
Servings: 8

Ingredients:

- 1 lb kangaroo sausage meat
- 2 sheets puff pastry, thawed
- 1 egg, beaten (for egg wash)
- Tomato chutney for dipping

Instructions:

1. Preheat the oven to 190°C (375°F).
2. Spread the puff pastry sheets out.
3. Slice the meat from the kangaroo sausage in half, then roll every half into logs along the length of the pastry sheet.
4. Seal the edges by folding the pastry over the sausage meat.
5. Apply a beaten egg glaze for a golden appearance.
6. Divide the rolls into minier portions.
7. Put in the oven for 20 to 25 mins, or up to golden brown, on a baking sheet.
8. Accompany with a tomato chutney.
9. Savour your kangaroo sausage rolls with gusto!

Nutrition (per serving):

Cals: 300, Protein: 12g, Carbs: 15g, Fat: 20g

Fiber: 1g

16. Barramundi Tacos with Mango Salsa

Prep Time: 20 mins
Cook Time: 10 mins
Total Time: 30 mins
Servings: 4

Ingredients:

- 1 lb barramundi fillets
- 2 tbsp olive oil
- 1 tsp chili powder
- 1 tsp cumin
- 1/2 tsp garlic powder
- Salt and pepper as needed
- 8 mini tortillas
- 1 cup of shredded cabbage
- 1 mango, diced
- 1/4 cup of red onion, lightly chop-up
- 1/4 cup of fresh cilantro, chop-up
- 1 lime, juiced

Instructions:

1. Heat the pan or grill to a medium-high temperature.
2. Mix olive oil, salt, pepper, cumin, garlic powder, and chilli powder in a bowl.
3. Use the spice mixture to lightly coat the barramundi fillets.
4. Barramundi Must be cooked through after grilling for 3–4 mins on every side.
5. Grilled tortillas are warm.
6. To make the salsa, mix the chop-up red onion, chop-up cilantro, diced mango, shredded cabbage, and lime juice in a separate bowl.

7. After grilling, cut up the barramundi and arrange it over the tortillas.
8. Add mango salsa on top.
9. Present your barramundi tacos and savour them!

Cals: 350, Protein: 20g, Carbs: 30g, Fat: 15g
Fiber: 5g

17. Australian Barramundi Ceviche

Prep Time: 15 mins
Marination Time: 2 hrs
Total Time: 2 hrs 15 mins
Servings: 4

Ingredients:
- 1 lb barramundi fillets, thinly split
- 1/2 cup of lime juice
- 1/4 cup of lemon juice
- 1/4 cup of orange juice
- 1 cucumber, diced
- 1/2 red onion, lightly chop-up
- 1/4 cup of fresh cilantro, chop-up
- 1 jalapeño, seeded and chop-up
- Salt and pepper as needed
- Avocado slices for garnish
- Tortilla chips for serving

Instructions:
1. Mix the orange, lemon, and lime juices in a bowl.
2. Slice the barramundi thinly and add it to the citrus juice mixture.
3. To marinate, cover and chill for a minimum of two hrs.
4. Mix split cucumber, chop-up jalapeño, lightly chop-up red onion, chop-up cilantro, and salt and pepper in a separate bowl.
5. Fold the marinated barramundi gently into the cucumber mixture.
6. Arrange the barramundi ceviche into bowls and top with split avocado.
7. Savour your tortilla chips and Australian barramundi ceviche!

Nutrition (per serving):
Cals: 200, Protein: 25g, Carbs: 10g, Fat: 8g, Fiber: 3g

18. Vegemite and Cheese Scrolls

Prep Time: 15 mins
Cook Time: 20 mins
Total Time: 35 mins
Servings: 12

Ingredients:
- 2 1/2 cups of self-raising flour
- 1 cup of milk
- 1/4 cup of butter, dilute
- 1/4 cup of Vegemite
- 1 1/2 cups of finely grated cheese (cheddar or your choice)

Instructions:
1. Turn the oven on to 425°F (220°C) and coat a baking dish with oil.
2. To make a dough, mix milk and self-raising flour in a bowl.
3. On a surface dusted with flour, roll out the dough to form a rectangle.
4. Evenly distribute Vegemite over the dough.
5. Over the Vegemite, scatter the finely grated cheese.
6. To form a log, tightly roll the dough starting from the longer side.
7. 12 slices of the log Must be slice and put in the baking dish that has been oiled.
8. Melt the butter and brush every scroll's top.
9. Bake up to golden brown, about 20 mins.

Nutrition:
Cals: 200 per serving, Protein: 5g, Carbs: 25g
Fat: 8g, Fiber: 1g

19. Bush Tomato and Pepperberry Chicken

Prep Time: 15 mins
Cook Time: 25 mins
Total Time: 40 mins
Servings: 4

Ingredients:
- 4 boneless, skinless chicken breasts
- 2 tbsp bush tomato chutney
- 1 tsp ground pepperberry
- 1 tbsp olive oil
- Salt as needed
- Fresh parsley for garnish

Instructions:
1. Preheat the oven to 190°C (375°F).
2. Salt is used to season chicken breasts.
3. Mix olive oil, ground pepperberry, and bush tomato chutney in a bowl.
4. Turn every chicken breast over and coat with mixture.
5. The chicken breasts Must be put on a baking dish.
6. Bake the chicken for 25 mins, or up to it is thoroughly done.
7. Before serving, garnish with fresh parsley.

Nutrition:

Cals: 250 per serving, Protein: 30g, Carbs: 5g

Fat: 12g, Fiber: 1g

20. Quandong Glazed Duck Breast

Prep Time: 10 mins
Cook Time: 20 mins
Total Time: 30 mins
Servings: 2

Ingredients:

- 2 duck breasts
- Salt and pepper as needed
- 1/2 cup of quandong jam
- 2 tbsp balsamic vinegar
- Fresh thyme for garnish

Instructions:

1. Set oven temperature to 400°F, or 200°C.
2. Duck breasts Must have their skin scored and seasoned with salt and pepper.
3. Mix quandong jam and balsamic vinegar in a bowl.
4. Apply the quandong glaze to the duck breasts.
5. The duck breasts Must be put on a baking dish.
6. Roast the duck for 20 mins, or up to it's cooked to your preference and the skin is crispy.
7. Before serving, garnish with freshly slice thyme.

Nutrition:

Cals: 400 per serving, Protein: 25g, Carbs: 20g, Fat: 25g, Fiber: 2g

21. Pumpkin Scone Damper

Prep Time: 15 mins
Cook Time: 25 mins
Total Time: 40 mins
Servings: 8

Ingredients:

- 3 cups of self-raising flour
- 1 tsp salt
- 1 cup of mashed pumpkin
- 1/2 cup of butter, dilute
- 1/2 cup of milk

Instructions:

1. Warm up the oven to 400°F, or 200°C, and coat a baking sheet with oil.
2. Mix salt and self-raising flour in a bowl.
3. Add milk, dilute butter, and mashed pumpkin. Blend up to barely combined.
4. After transferring the dough to a floured board, form it into a round damper.
5. After greasing the baking sheet, place the damper on it.
6. Make a cross-strike on the damper's top with a sharp knife.
7. Bake up to the damper is golden brown, about 25 mins.

Nutrition:

Cals: 300 per serving, Protein: 5g, Carbs: 40g

Fat: 12g, Fiber: 2g

22. Lemon Myrtle Chicken Skewers

Prep Time: 15 mins
Cook Time: 10 mins
Total Time: 25 mins
Servings: 4

Ingredients:

- 1 lb chicken breast, slice into cubes
- 2 tbsp olive oil
- 2 tbsp lemon myrtle seasoning
- Salt and pepper as needed
- Wooden skewers, soaked in water
- Lemon wedges for serving

Instructions:

1. Turn the heat up to medium-high on the grill or grill pan.
2. Toss the chicken cubes in a basin with the olive oil, salt, pepper, and lemon myrtle seasoning.
3. After soaking the wooden skewers, thread the marinated chicken onto them.
4. Cook the chicken for 5 mins on every side, or up to it is thoroughly cooked.
5. Accompany with wedges of lemon.

Nutrition:

Cals: 200 per serving, Protein: 25g, Carbs: 2g

Fat: 10g, Fiber: 1g

23. Grilled Prawns with Finger Lime

Prep Time: 15 mins
Cook Time: 5 mins
Total Time: 20 mins
Servings: 4

Ingredients:

- 1 lb Big prawns, peel off and deveined
- 2 tbsp olive oil
- 2 cloves garlic, chop-up
- 1 tsp finger lime pearls
- Salt and pepper as needed
- Fresh cilantro for garnish

Instructions:

1. Turn the heat up to high on the grill or grill pan.
2. Toss the prawns in a basin with the olive oil, finger lime pearls, chop-up garlic, salt, and pepper.
3. Put the prawns through skewers.
4. Grill the prawns for two to three mins on every side, or up to they are cooked through and opaque.
5. Before serving, garnish with fresh cilantro.

Nutrition:

Cals: 150 per serving, Protein: 20g, Carbs: 1g
Fat: 8g, Fiber: 1g

24. Wattleseed and Honey Ice Cream

Prep Time: 10 mins
Churning Time: 20 mins
Total Time: 30 mins
Servings: 6

Ingredients:

- 2 cups of heavy cream
- 1 cup of whole milk
- 3/4 cup of honey
- 2 tbsp ground roasted wattleseed
- 1 tsp vanilla extract

Instructions:

1. Pour the whole milk and heavy cream into a saucepan and heat over medium heat up to the mixture starts to steam; do not boil.
2. Mix honey, vanilla extract, and ground roasted wattleseed in a bowl.
3. While whisking continuously, slowly pour the honey mixture into the heated milk mixture.
4. Place the mixture in the refrigerator to chill fully.
5. Following the manufacturer's instructions, churn the mixture in an ice cream machine when it has cooled.
6. When the ice cream has thickened, transfer it to a container with a lid and freeze it for at least four hrs.

Nutrition:

Cals: 300 per serving, Protein: 3g, Carbs: 30g
Fat: 20g, Fiber: 1g

25. Aussie Breakfast Stack

Prep Time: 15 mins
Cook Time: 15 mins
Total Time: 30 mins
Servings: 2

Ingredients:

- 4 slices bacon
- 2 Big eggs
- 2 English muffins, toasted
- 1 avocado, split
- 1 tomato, split
- Salt and pepper as needed
- Chop-up chives for garnish

Instructions:

1. Crisp up the bacon in a skillet. Take out and place aside.
2. Fry the eggs to your taste in the same skillet.
3. Toasted English muffins Must be arranged on a platter before assembling the breakfast stack.
4. Add pieces of avocado, tomato, bacon, and fried egg on top of every muffin.
5. Add pepper and salt for seasoning.
6. Sprinkle chop-up chives over top.
7. Your Aussie breakfast stack is ready to eat!

Nutrition (per serving):

Cals: 500, Protein: 20g, Carbs: 30g, Fat: 35g, Fiber: 8g

26. Barramundi with Lemon Myrtle Butter

Prep Time: 10 mins
Cook Time: 15 mins
Total Time: 25 mins
Servings: 4

Ingredients:

- 4 barramundi fillets
- 2 tbsp olive oil
- 2 tbsp lemon myrtle leaves, lightly chop-up
- 4 tbsp unsalted butter
- 1 lemon, split
- Salt and pepper as needed
- Fresh parsley for garnish

Instructions:

1. Set oven temperature to 400°F, or 200°C.
2. Rub some salt and pepper on the barramundi fillets.
3. Heat the olive oil in a skillet that is ovensafe to medium-high heat.
4. Marinate barramundi fillets for two to three mins on every side.
5. Melt butter in a mini pot and add chop-up lemon myrtle leaves.
6. Cover the barramundi fillets with butter made with lemon myrtle.
7. Top with slices of lemon.
8. After placing the pan in the oven, bake it for ten mins, or up to the fish is thoroughly cooked.
9. Add fresh parsley as a garnish.

10. Present and relish your barramundi with butter made from lemon myrtle!

Nutrition (per serving):
Cals: 300, Protein: 25g, Carbs: 1g
Fat: 20g, Fiber: 0g

27. Vegemite and Cheese Stuffed Mushrooms

Prep Time: 15 mins
Cook Time: 20 mins
Total Time: 35 mins
Servings: 4

Ingredients:

- 12 Big mushrooms, cleaned and stems take outd
- 1/4 cup of Vegemite
- 1/2 cup of cream cheese
- 1 cup of shredded cheddar cheese
- 2 tbsp olive oil
- Fresh parsley for garnish

Instructions:

1. Preheat the oven to 190°C (375°F).
2. Mix shredded cheddar cheese, cream cheese, and Vegemite in a bowl.
3. Stuff the cheese and Vegemite mixture inside every mushroom cap.
4. Stuffed mushrooms ought to be put on a baking pan.
5. Olive oil Must be drizzled on the mushrooms.
6. Bake the mushrooms for 20 mins, or up to they are soft.
7. Add fresh parsley as a garnish.
8. Present and savour your cheese-filled mushrooms with Vegemite!

Nutrition (per serving):
Cals: 200, Protein: 8g, Carbs: 5g, Fat: 15g
Fiber: 1g

28. Pepperberry Kangaroo Burgers

Prep Time: 20 mins
Cook Time: 10 mins
Total Time: 30 mins
Servings: 4

Ingredients:

- 1 lb ground kangaroo meat
- 1 tbsp ground pepperberry (or black pepper)
- 1 tsp garlic powder
- 1 tsp onion powder
- Salt as needed
- 4 burger buns
- Lettuce, tomato, and other toppings of choice
- Cheese slices (non-compulsory)
- Sauce of choice (e.g., aioli, barbecue sauce)

Instructions:

1. Mix the ground pepperberry, onion, and garlic powders, salt, and kangaroo meat in a bowl.
2. Form four patties out of the mixture.
3. Heat the pan or grill to a medium-high temperature.
4. After 4-5 mins on every side, or up to done to your preference, grill the kangaroo patties.
5. On the grill, toast the hamburger buns.
6. Add lettuce, tomato, cheese (if using), and sauce to the burgers.
7. Your pepperberry kangaroo burgers are ready to eat!

Nutrition (per serving):
Cals: 300, Protein: 25g, Carbs: 25g, Fat: 12g
Fiber: 2g

29. Damper Bread and Golden Syrup Butter

Prep Time: 15 mins
Cook Time: 25 mins
Total Time: 40 mins
Servings: 6

Ingredients:

- 3 cups of self-rising flour
- 1 tsp salt
- 1 cup of milk
- 2 tbsp golden syrup
- 1/2 cup of unsalted butter, melted

Instructions:

1. Preheat the oven to 190°C (375°F).
2. Mix salt and self-rising flour in a bowl.
3. To make a soft dough, stir in the golden syrup and milk.
4. Utilising a floured surface, knead the dough.
5. Create a circular loaf out of the dough.
6. Scratch the top of the loaf and place it on a baking pan.
7. Bake up to the damper sounds hollow when tapped, 20 to 25 mins.
8. Mix golden syrup and melted butter in a bowl.
9. Serve the butter with golden syrup alongside the damper bread.
10. Savour your butter with golden syrup and damper bread!

Nutrition (per serving):
Cals: 350, Protein: 6g, Carbs: 50g, Fat: 15g

Fiber: 1g

30. Macadamia-Crusted Chicken Tenders

Prep Time: 15 mins
Cook Time: 15 mins
Total Time: 30 mins
Servings: 4

Ingredients:

- 1 lb chicken tenders
- 1 cup of macadamia nuts, lightly chop-up
- 1/2 cup of breadcrumbs
- 2 eggs, beaten
- Salt and pepper as needed
- Olive oil for frying
- Lemon wedges for serving

Instructions:

1. Preheat the oven to 190°C (375°F).
2. Add salt and pepper to chicken tenders for seasoning.
3. Place breadcrumbs and chop-up macadamia nuts in a shlet dish.
4. Coat every chicken tender in a combination of breadcrumbs and macadamia nuts after dipping it into beaten eggs.
5. In a skillet that is ovensafe, warm the olive oil over medium-high heat.
6. Chicken tenders Must be browned on all sides.
7. After placing the pan in the oven, roast it for ten to twelve mins, or up to the chicken is thoroughly cooked.
8. Accompany with wedges of lemon.
9. Savour your chicken tenders with a macadamia crust!

Nutrition (per serving):

Cals: 400, Protein: 25g, Carbs: 15g, Fat: 30g
Fiber: 2g

31. Salt and Pepper Squid

Prep Time: 15 mins
Cook Time: 5 mins
Total Time: 20 mins
Servings: 4

Ingredients:

- 1 lb squid tubes, cleaned and split into rings
- 1/2 cup of cornstarch
- 1 tsp sea salt
- 1 tsp black pepper
- Vegetable oil for frying
- Lemon wedges for serving

Instructions:

1. Mix cornflour, sea salt, and black pepper in a bowl.
2. In a big pot or deep fryer, heat the vegetable oil to 350°F (175°C).
3. Coat the squid rings equally by tossing them in the cornflour mixture.
4. Fry squid in batches for one to two mins, or up to crisp and golden brown.
5. blot with paper towels.
6. Accompany with wedges of lemon.
7. Savour the squid with salt & pepper!

Nutrition (per serving):

Cals: 250, Protein: 20g, Carbs: 15g, Fat: 12g
Fiber: 1g

32. Kangaroo Chili Con Carne

Prep Time: 15 mins
Cook Time: 30 mins
Total Time: 45 mins
Servings: 6

Ingredients:

- 1 lb kangaroo meat, chop-up
- 1 onion, chop-up
- 2 cloves garlic, chop-up
- 1 red bell pepper, diced
- 14 ounces (one can) of rinsed and drained kidney beans
- 1 can (14 oz) diced tomatoes
- 2 tbsp tomato paste
- 2 tbsp chili powder
- 1 tsp ground cumin
- 1 tsp smoked paprika
- Salt and pepper as needed
- Olive oil for cooking
- Chop-up fresh cilantro for garnish
- Shredded cheese for topping (non-compulsory)
- Sour cream for serving (non-compulsory)

Instructions:

1. Warm up the olive oil in a big pot over medium heat.
2. Add chop-up garlic and diced onions. Onions Must be sautéed up to transparent.
3. Cook the kangaroo meat up to it turns brown.
4. Add the smoked paprika, kidney beans, chop-up tomatoes, diced bell pepper, tomato paste, chilli powder, and powdered cumin.
5. Simmer for twenty to twenty-five mins, stirring now and then.
6. Taste and adjust the seasoning.

7. Garnish with chop-up cilantro and serve hot. Add some shredded cheese on top if desired, and serve with sour cream.

Nutrition:
Cals: 300 per serving, Protein: 25g, Carbs: 20g
Fat: 12g, Fiber: 6g

33.Aussie Lamb Chops with Mint Sauce

Prep Time: 10 mins
Cook Time: 15 mins
Total Time: 25 mins
Servings: 4

Ingredients:
- 8 Aussie lamb chops
- Salt and pepper as needed
- Olive oil for grilling
- Fresh mint leaves for garnish
- Mint Sauce:
- 1/2 cup of fresh mint leaves, lightly chop-up
- 2 tbsp white wine vinegar
- 1 tbsp sugar
- Salt as needed

Instructions:
1. Turn the heat up to medium-high on the grill or grill pan.
2. Salt and pepper are used to season lamb chops.
3. Lamb chops Must be cooked to your preference after grilling for 5 to 7 mins on every side.
4. To make the mint sauce, mix the chop-up mint, white wine vinegar, sugar, and salt in a mini bowl.
5. Serve lamb chops hot with fresh mint leaves as a garnish and a sprinkle of mint sauce.

Nutrition:
Cals: 400 per serving, Protein: 30g, Carbs: 2g
Fat: 30g, Fiber: 1g

34.Aussie Pumpkin Soup

Prep Time: 15 mins
Cook Time: 30 mins
Total Time: 45 mins
Servings: 6

Ingredients:
- 1 kg pumpkin, peel off and diced
- 1 onion, chop-up
- 2 carrots, peel off and split
- 2 potatoes, peel off and diced
- 4 cups of vegetable broth
- 1 cup of coconut milk
- 1 tsp ground cumin

- 1 tsp ground coriander
- Salt and pepper as needed
- Olive oil for cooking
- Fresh chives for garnish

Instructions:
1. Warm up the olive oil in a big pot over medium heat.
2. Saute the split onions till they become transparent.
3. Add the chop-up potatoes, split carrots, and diced pumpkin. For a few mins, stir.
4. After adding the veggie broth, bring it to a boil. Vegetables Must be simmered till soft.
5. Puree the soup with an immersion blender or blender up to it's smooth.
6. Add the ground coriander, cumin, and pepper to the coconut milk and stir. Simmer for five more mins.
7. Taste and adjust the seasoning.
8. Garnish with fresh chives and serve hot.

Nutrition:
Cals: 250 per serving, Protein: 3g, Carbs: 30g
Fat: 15g, Fiber: 5g

35.Barramundi with Bush Tomato Relish

Prep Time: 10 mins
Cook Time: 15 mins
Total Time: 25 mins
Servings: 4

Ingredients:
- 4 barramundi fillets
- Salt and pepper as needed
- Olive oil for cooking
- Bush tomato relish for serving
- Bush Tomato Relish:
- 1/2 cup of bush tomatoes, rehydrated and chop-up
- 1 onion, lightly chop-up
- 2 cloves garlic, chop-up
- 1/4 cup of red wine vinegar
- 2 tbsp brown sugar
- 1 tbsp olive oil

Instructions:
1. Rub some salt and pepper on the barramundi fillets.
2. In a skillet set over medium heat, warm the olive oil.
3. Barramundi fillets Must be cooked thoroughly after 3–4 mins on every side.
4. Rehydrated and chop-up bush tomatoes, lightly chop-up onion, chop-up garlic, red wine vinegar,

brown sugar, and olive oil Must all be mixd in a bowl to make the bush tomato relish. Blend thoroughly.

5. Top the warm barramundi with a relish made from bush tomatoes.

Nutrition:

Cals: 300 per serving, Protein: 25g, Carbs: 10g

Fat: 15g, Fiber: 2g

36.Crocodile Satay Skewers

Prep Time: 20 mins
Cook Time: 10 mins
Total Time: 30 mins
Servings: 4

Ingredients:

- 1 lb crocodile meat, slice into cubes
- 1/2 cup of coconut milk
- 2 tbsp soy sauce
- 1 tbsp honey
- 1 tbsp peanut butter
- 2 cloves garlic, chop-up
- 1 tsp ground coriander
- Wooden skewers, soaked in water
- Chop-up peanuts and fresh cilantro for garnish

Instructions:

1. To make the marinade, mix the coconut milk, ground coriander, honey, soy sauce, peanut butter, and chop-up garlic in a bowl.
2. Cubes of crocodile meat Must be added to the marinade and left for at least fifteen mins.
3. Marinate the crocodile cubes and thread them onto the wet wooden skewers.
4. Skewers Must be cooked through after 4–5 mins on every side of the grill.
5. Before serving, garnish with chop-up peanuts and fresh cilantro.

Nutrition:

Cals: 200 per serving, Protein: 20g, Carbs: 10g

Fat: 10g, Fiber: 1g

37.Vegemite and Cheese Frittata

Prep Time: 15 mins
Cook Time: 20 mins
Total Time: 35 mins
Servings: 6

Ingredients:

- 8 eggs
- 1/4 cup of milk
- 2 tbsp Vegemite
- 1 cup of finely grated cheese (cheddar or your choice)
- 1 onion, chop-up
- 1 bell pepper, diced
- 1 cup of cherry tomatoes, halved
- Salt and pepper as needed
- Olive oil for cooking
- Fresh parsley for garnish

Instructions:

1. Preheat the oven to 190°C (375°F).
2. Beat the eggs, milk, and Vegemite together thoroughly in a bowl.
3. Add the split bell pepper, chop-up onion, finely grated cheese, and cherry tomatoes slice in half. Add pepper and salt for seasoning.
4. Heat the olive oil in a skillet that is ovensafe to medium.
5. Transfer the beaten eggs into the skillet.
6. Cook up to the edges start to set, 3 to 4 mins on the hob.
7. Place the skillet in the oven that has been preheated, and bake for 15 to 20 mins, or up to the frittata is golden and thoroughly cooked.
8. Before serving, garnish with fresh parsley.

Nutrition:

Cals: 250 per serving, Protein: 15g, Carbs: 5g

Fat: 18g, Fiber: 2g

38.Kakadu Plum Glazed Quail

Prep Time: 15 mins
Cook Time: 20 mins
Total Time: 35 mins
Servings: 4

Ingredients:

- 4 quails, halved
- Salt and pepper as needed
- 1/2 cup of Kakadu plum jam
- 2 tbsp balsamic vinegar
- 1 tbsp olive oil
- Fresh thyme for garnish

Instructions:

1. Preheat the oven to 190°C (375°F).
2. Sprinkle some salt and pepper on the quail halves.
3. Heat the olive oil, balsamic vinegar, and Kakadu plum jam in a mini saucepan over low heat. Mix thoroughly up to fully incorporated.
4. Drizzle the plum glaze over the quail halves.
5. Put the halves of quail into a baking tray and bake for 15 to 20 mins, or up to they are cooked through.

6. Brush with extra plum glaze while you roast.
7. Before serving, garnish with freshly slice thyme.

Nutrition:
Cals: 300 per serving, Protein: 20g, Carbs: 15g

Fat: 15g, Fiber: 1g

39. Wattleseed Anzac Biscuits

Prep Time: 15 mins
Baking Time: 12 mins
Total Time: 27 mins
Servings: 24 biscuits

Ingredients:
- 1 cup of rolled oats
- 1 cup of desiccated coconut
- 1 cup of all-purpose flour
- 1 cup of brown sugar
- 1/2 cup of wattleseed
- 150g (5.3 oz) unsalted butter, dilute
- 2 tbsp golden syrup
- 1/2 tsp baking soda
- 2 tbsp boiling water

Instructions:
1. Set oven temperature to 325°F, or 160°C. Cooking sheets should be lined with parchment paper.
2. All-purpose flour, brown sugar, wattleseed, desiccated coconut, and rolled oats Must be mixd in a big basin.
3. Melt butter and golden syrup Must be added after mixing baking soda and boiling water in an other basin.
4. After adding the wet ingredients to the dry ingredients, thoroughly mix them together.
5. Leaving room between every drop of the mixture, place spoonfuls onto the baking sheets that have been prepared.
6. Bake till golden brown, 12 mins or so.
7. Before moving the Anzac cookies to a wire rack, let them cool on the baking sheets.
8. Savour your Anzac Biscuits with Wattleseed!

Nutrition (per serving):
Cals: 150, Protein: 2g, Carbs: 18g

Fat: 8g, Fiber: 1g

40. Aussie Meat Lover's Pizza

Prep Time: 20 mins
Cook Time: 15 mins
Total Time: 35 mins
Servings: 4

Ingredients:
- 1 pizza dough (store-bought or homemade)
- 1/2 cup of tomato sauce
- 1 cup of shredded mozzarella cheese
- 1/2 cup of cooked kangaroo meat, shredded
- 1/2 cup of cooked beef strips
- 1/4 cup of cooked bacon, cut up
- 1/4 cup of split pepperoni
- 1/4 cup of split ham
- 1/4 cup of split chorizo
- 1/4 cup of split mushrooms
- 1/4 cup of split red onions
- Fresh basil leaves for garnish

Instructions:
1. As directed on the pizza dough packaging, preheat the oven to that temperature.
2. On a surface dusted with flour, roll out the pizza dough to the appropriate thickness.
3. Over the pizza crust, equally distribute the tomato sauce.
4. On top of the sauce, scatter the mozzarella cheese.
5. Scatter the kangaroo meat, beef strips, red onions, mushrooms, chorizo, bacon, pepperoni and ham over the pizza.
6. Bake in the preheated oven up to the cheese is dilute and bubbling and the crust is brown, following the directions on the pizza dough.
7. Take it out of the oven, top with some fresh basil leaves, and let it to cool for a little while.
8. Enjoy your Aussie Meat Lover's Pizza after slicing it!

Nutrition (per serving):
Cals: 400, Protein: 20g, Carbs: 30g

Fat: 22g, Fiber: 2g

41. Kangaroo and Sweet Potato Pie

Prep Time: 20 mins
Cook Time: 40 mins
Total Time: 1 hr
Servings: 6

Ingredients:
- 1 lb kangaroo meat, diced
- 2 tbsp olive oil
- 1 onion, diced
- 2 cloves garlic, chop-up
- 1 cup of sweet potato, diced and cooked
- 1 cup of refrigerate peas
- One cup of vegetable or beef broth
- 2 tbsp tomato paste
- 1 tsp dried thyme

- Salt and pepper as needed
- 1 sheet puff pastry, thawed
- 1 egg, beaten (for egg wash)

Instructions:

1. Preheat the oven to 190°C (375°F).
2. Heat up some olive oil in a pan and fry some chop-up kangaroo meat up to it turns brown. Take out and place aside.
3. Saute chop-up onions in the same pan up to they become transparent. Add the chop-up garlic and continue cooking for one more min.
4. Add the sweet potato, refrigerate peas, tomato paste, dried thyme, broth, salt, and pepper to the pan with the kangaroo meat after it has been returned. Simmer for ten mins.
5. Spoon the mixture into an ovenproof dish.
6. After rolling out the puff pastry and Cutting off any excess, cover the filling.
7. To give the pastry a golden sheen, brush it with beaten egg.
8. Bake the pastry for 30 to 40 mins, or up to it becomes brown and puffy.
9. Before serving, let the pie to cool somewhat.
10. Savour your sweet potato pie and kangaroo!

Nutrition (per serving):

Cals: 350, Protein: 18g, Carbs: 25g

Fat: 20g, Fiber: 4g

42.Grilled Barramundi Tacos

Prep Time: 20 mins
Cook Time: 10 mins
Total Time: 30 mins
Servings: 4

Ingredients:

- 1 lb barramundi fillets
- 2 tbsp olive oil
- 1 tsp chili powder
- 1 tsp cumin
- 1/2 tsp garlic powder
- Salt and pepper as needed
- 8 mini tortillas
- 1 cup of shredded cabbage
- 1 mango, diced
- 1/4 cup of red onion, lightly chop-up
- 1/4 cup of fresh cilantro, chop-up
- 1 lime, juiced

Instructions:

1. Heat the pan or grill to a medium-high temperature.
2. Mix olive oil, salt, pepper, cumin, garlic powder, and chilli powder in a bowl.

3. Use the spice mixture to lightly coat the barramundi fillets.
4. Barramundi Must be cooked through after grilling for 3–4 mins on every side.
5. Grilled tortillas are warm.
6. To make the salsa, mix the chop-up red onion, chop-up cilantro, diced mango, shredded cabbage, and lime juice in a separate bowl.
7. After grilling, cut up the barramundi and arrange it over the tortillas.
8. Add mango salsa on top.
9. Get your barramundi tacos served and enjoy!

Nutrition (per serving):

Cals: 350, Protein: 20g, Carbs: 30g

Fat: 15g, Fiber: 5g

43.Tim Tam Cheesecake

Prep Time: 20 mins
Chilling Time: 4 hrs
Total Time: 4 hrs 20 mins
Servings: 8

Ingredients:

- 2 cups of Tim Tam cookies, crushed
- 1/2 cup of unsalted butter, dilute
- 24 oz cream cheese, melted
- 1 cup of granulated sugar
- 1 tsp vanilla extract
- 4 Big eggs
- 1 cup of sour cream
- 1/4 cup of all-purpose flour
- 1/2 cup of chocolate sauce (for drizzling)
- Tim Tam cookies for garnish

Instructions:

1. Set the oven temperature to 325°F (163°C). In a 9-inch springform pan, grease it.
2. Melt butter and crushed Tim Tam cookies in a bowl.
3. To make the crust, press the cookie mixture firmly into the bottom of the springform pan that has been prepped.
4. Beat cream cheese, sugar, and vanilla extract together up to smooth in a sizable mixing dish.
5. Beat thoroughly after every addition of egg. Add eggs one at a time.
6. Just blend the flour and sour cream by folding them in.
7. Over the crust in the springform pan, pour the cream cheese mixture.
8. Bake up to the centre is firm, about 50 to 60 mins.

9. After letting the cheesecake cool, chill it in the refrigerator for four or more hrs or overnight.
10. Before serving, drizzle some chocolate sauce over the top and add more Tim Tam cookies as a garnish.
11. Savour your cheesecake with Tim Tams!

Nutrition (per serving):
Cals: 500, Protein: 8g, Carbs: 45g, Fat: 35g, Fiber: 1g

44. Australian Beef and Guinness Stew

Prep Time: 20 mins
Cook Time: 2 hrs
Total Time: 2 hrs 20 mins
Servings: 6

Ingredients:

- 2 lbs beef stew meat, cubed
- Salt and pepper as needed
- 2 tbsp olive oil
- 1 Big onion, chop-up
- 2 cloves garlic, chop-up
- 2 tbsp all-purpose flour
- 1 can (14 oz) Guinness beer
- 2 cups of beef broth
- 2 tbsp tomato paste
- 1 tbsp Worcestershire sauce
- 1 tsp dried thyme
- 4 carrots, peel off and split
- 2 potatoes, peel off and cubed
- Fresh parsley for garnish

Instructions:

1. Use salt and pepper to season the beef stew meat.
2. Warm up the olive oil in a big pot over medium-high heat.
3. Batch-brown the beef and set aside.
4. Add the chop-up onions to the pot and sauté up to they soften. Add the chop-up garlic and continue cooking for one more min.
5. Toss to coat the onions and garlic with the flour.
6. Pour in the Guinness beer, scraping up any browned bits from the pot's bottom.
7. After the beef has browned again, add the tomato paste, Worcestershire sauce, dried thyme, and beef broth to the pot. Heat through to a simmer.
8. Put potatoes and carrots in the pot. Once the beef is cooked, simmer it covered for one and a half to two hrs.
9. If necessary, adjust the spice and add fresh parsley as a garnish.
10. Present your Guinness Stew and Australian Beef!

Nutrition (per serving):
Cals: 400, Protein: 30g, Carbs: 20g, Fat: 20g, Fiber: 4g

45. Lamington French Toast

Prep Time: 15 mins
Cook Time: 10 mins
Total Time: 25 mins
Servings: 4

Ingredients:

- 8 slices day-old white bread
- 3 eggs
- 1 cup of milk
- 1/4 cup of unsweetened cocoa powder
- 1/4 cup of granulated sugar
- 1 tsp vanilla extract
- Butter for frying
- Shredded coconut for coating
- Raspberry jam for serving

Instructions:

1. Whisk together eggs, milk, sugar, vanilla extract, and cocoa powder in a mini bowl.
2. Coat both sides of every slice of bread by dipping it into the mixture.
3. In a frying pan, melt butter over medium heat.
4. Fry every slice up to both sides are golden brown.
5. Take out of the pan and cover right away with shredded coconut.
6. Present with a mound of raspberry jam on top.
7. Savour your French toast with Lamingtons!

Nutrition (per serving):
Cals: 350, Protein: 10g, Carbs: 40g, Fat: 18g
Fiber: 3g

46. Chicken Parmigiana with Tomato Chutney

Prep Time: 15 mins
Cook Time: 25 mins
Total Time: 40 mins
Servings: 4

Ingredients:

- 4 boneless, skinless chicken breasts
- Salt and pepper as needed
- 1 cup of all-purpose flour
- 2 eggs, beaten
- 1 cup of breadcrumbs
- 1/2 cup of Parmesan cheese that has been finely grated
- 2 tbsp olive oil
- 1 cup of tomato chutney

- 1 cup of shredded mozzarella cheese
- Fresh basil leaves for garnish

Instructions:

1. Preheat the oven to 190°C (375°F).
2. Add salt and pepper to chicken breasts for seasoning.
3. Every chicken breast Must be coated with a mixture of breadcrumbs and finely grated Parmesan cheese after being dredged in flour and dipped in beaten eggs.
4. Heat the olive oil in a pan over medium-high heat. Chicken breasts Must be browned on both sides.
5. Place the chicken in a baking dish after it has browned.
6. Drizzle every chicken breast with chutney made of tomatoes.
7. Add shredded mozzarella cheese on top.
8. Bake for 20 to 25 mins, or up to the cheese is dilute and bubbling, and the chicken is thoroughly cooked.
9. Add some fresh basil leaves as garnish.
10. Serve Tomato Chutney alongside your Chicken Parmigiana!

Nutrition (per serving):

Cals: 400, Protein: 30g, Carbs: 25g, Fat: 20g

Fiber: 2g

47.Bush Tomato Lamb Shanks

Prep Time: 20 mins
Cook Time: 3 hrs
Total Time: 3 hrs and 20 mins
Servings: 4

Ingredients:

- 4 lamb shanks
- 2 tbsp olive oil
- 1 onion, chop-up
- 2 carrots, split
- 2 celery stalks, chop-up
- 3 cloves garlic, chop-up
- 2 tbsp bush tomato chutney
- 1 cup of red wine
- 2 cups of beef or vegetable broth
- 1 can (14 oz) diced tomatoes
- 2 bay leaves
- Salt and pepper as needed
- Fresh parsley for garnish

Instructions:

1. Set the oven temperature to 325°F (163°C).
2. Heat the olive oil in a Big ovenproof pot over medium-high heat.

3. Shanks of lamb, brown on all sides. Take out and place aside.
4. Chop the celery, carrots, and onion and sauté them in the same saucepan up to they are soft.
5. Stir the bush tomato chutney and chop-up garlic for one to two mins.
6. Pour in the red wine, scraping out any browned bits from the pot's bottom.
7. Return the lamb shanks to the pot. Add the diced tomatoes and broth.
8. Season with salt and pepper and add the bay leaves.
9. Place the pot in the oven that has been warmed, covered.
10. Bake the lamb for 2.5 to 3 hrs, or up to it is soft.
11. Before serving, garnish with fresh parsley.

Nutrition:

Cals: 400 per serving, Protein: 30g, Carbs: 15g

Fat: 25g, Fiber: 3g

48.Pumpkin and Macadamia Nut Risotto

Prep Time: 15 mins
Cook Time: 30 mins
Total Time: 45 mins
Servings: 6

Ingredients:

- 2 cups of Arborio rice
- 1/2 cup of macadamia nuts, chop-up
- 1 onion, lightly chop-up
- 2 cloves garlic, chop-up
- 1 cup of pumpkin, diced
- 6 cups of vegetable broth, kept warm
- 1/2 cup of dry white wine
- finely grated Parmesan cheese, half a cup
- 2 tbsp butter
- Salt and pepper as needed
- Fresh sage leaves for garnish

Instructions:

1. Toast the Arborio rice and chop-up macadamia nuts in a big skillet over medium heat up to they start to turn golden brown. Remove from the pan and set aside.
2. Lightly slice the onion and mince the garlic and sauté them in the same skillet up to they become tender.
3. Saute the diced pumpkin for a further two to three mins.
4. Add the dry white wine and whisk up to it is absorbed.

5. spoonful one spoonful of warm vegetable soup at a time, stirring up to it is absorbed before adding another.
6. This process Must be repeated up to the rice is cooked through and creamy.
7. Add the butter and finely grated Parmesan cheese and stir. Add pepper and salt for seasoning.
8. Before serving, garnish with fresh sage leaves.

Nutrition:
Cals: 350 per serving, Protein: 8g, Carbs: 60g
Fat: 10g, Fiber: 3g

49.Barramundi with Lemon Myrtle Crust

Prep Time: 15 mins
Cook Time: 15 mins
Total Time: 30 mins
Servings: 4

Ingredients:
- 4 barramundi fillets
- 1/2 cup of breadcrumbs
- 2 tbsp lemon myrtle seasoning
- Zest of 1 lemon
- Salt and pepper as needed
- 2 eggs, beaten
- Olive oil for cooking
- Lemon wedges for serving

Instructions:
1. Preheat the oven to 190°C (375°F).
2. Mix breadcrumbs, salt, pepper, lemon zest, and lemon myrtle seasoning in a bowl.
3. Barramundi fillets are coated with the breadcrumb mixture after being dipped into beaten eggs.
4. Heat the olive oil in a skillet that is ovensafe to medium-high heat.
5. Grill barramundi fillets till golden brown, two to three mins per side.
6. After transferring the pan to the preheated oven, bake the barramundi for a further 10 to 12 mins, or up to it is thoroughly cooked.
7. Serve hot, with lemon slices as a garnish.

Nutrition:
Cals: 300 per serving, Protein: 25g, Carbs: 15g
Fat: 15g, Fiber: 1g

50.Vegemite and Cheese Potato Skins

Prep Time: 20 mins
Cook Time: 40 mins
Total Time: 1 hr
Servings: 8

Ingredients:
- 4 Big potatoes, scrubbed and baked
- 2 tbsp butter, dilute
- 2 tbsp Vegemite
- 1 cup of shredded cheese (cheddar or your choice)
- Sour cream and chives for serving

Instructions:
1. Set oven temperature to 400°F, or 20C°C.
2. Halve the cooked potatoes lengthwise.
3. Take out the flesh, leaving the skins with a thin covering on them.
4. Dilute butter and Vegemite Must be thoroughly combined in a bowl.
5. Apply the Vegemite mixture inside every potato skin.
6. The potato skins Must be put on a baking pan.
7. Divide the cheese into shreds and cover every potato peel.
8. Bake the cheese for 20 to 25 mins, or up to it is bubbling and dilute.
9. Serve hot, garnished with chop-up chives and a dollop of sour cream.

Nutrition:
Cals: 200 per serving, Protein: 5g, Carbs: 25g, Fat: 10g,
Fiber: 3g

51.Wattleseed Anzac Slice

Prep Time: 15 mins
Cook Time: 20 mins
Total Time: 35 mins
Servings: 12

Ingredients:
- 1 cup of rolled oats
- 1 cup of desiccated coconut
- 1 cup of plain flour
- 1/2 cup of brown sugar
- 1/2 cup of golden syrup
- 1/2 cup of unsalted butter, dilute
- 1 tsp wattleseed
- 1/2 tsp baking soda

Instructions:
1. Adjust the oven temperature to 350°F (180°C) and place parchment paper in a baking dish.
2. Rolled oats, desiccated coconut, brown sugar, wattleseed, and plain flour Must all be mixd in a big basin.
3. Dilute butter and golden syrup Must be heated in a saucepan over low heat up to blended.

4. Add the baking soda to the butter mixture after dissolving it in 1 tbsp of boiling water in a mini basin.
5. Mix thoroughly after adding the liquid mixture to the dry components.
6. Smoothing the top, press the mixture into the baking dish that has been prepared.
7. Roast for 15 to 20 mins, or up to browned on top.
8. Let cool completely before slicing.

Nutrition:

Cals: 200 per serving, Protein: 2g, Carbs: 25g

Fat: 10g, Fiber: 2g

52. Kangaroo and Bush Tomato Skewers

Prep Time: 15 mins
Cook Time: 10 mins
Total Time: 25 mins
Servings: 4

Ingredients:

- 1 lb kangaroo meat, slice into cubes
- 1/4 cup of olive oil
- 2 tbsp bush tomato chutney
- 1 tbsp balsamic vinegar
- 1 tsp dried combined herbs
- Salt and pepper as needed
- Wooden skewers, soaked in water
- Lemon wedges for serving

Instructions:

1. Mix the olive oil, balsamic vinegar, dried combined herbs, salt, and pepper in a bowl along with the bush tomato chutney.
2. Cubes of kangaroo meat Must be added to the marinade and left for at least fifteen mins.
3. Skewers dipped in water are threaded with marinated kangaroo cubes.
4. Skewers Must be cooked through after 4–5 mins on every side of the grill.
5. Accompany with wedges of lemon.

Nutrition:

Cals: 250 per serving, Protein: 30g, Carbs: 5g

Fat: 12g, Fiber: 1g

53. Aussie Meatball Subs

Prep Time: 20 mins
Cook Time: 20 mins
Total Time: 40 mins
Servings: 6

Ingredients:

- 1 lb ground beef or kangaroo meat
- 1/2 cup of breadcrumbs
- Finely shredded Parmesan cheese, 1/4 cup
- 1 egg
- 2 cloves garlic, chop-up
- 1 tsp dried oregano
- Salt and pepper as needed
- 1 cup of marinara sauce
- 6 sub rolls
- 1 cup of shredded mozzarella cheese
- Fresh basil for garnish

Instructions:

1. Preheat the oven to 190°C (375°F).
2. Ground beef, breadcrumbs, egg, finely grated Parmesan cheese, chop-up garlic, dried oregano, salt, and pepper Must all be mixd in a bowl. Blend up to thoroughly blended.
3. Place the meatballs you formed from the mixture onto a baking sheet.
4. Meatballs Must be baked for 15 to 20 mins, or up to done.
5. In a saucepan, warm the marinara sauce.
6. Dividing the subrolls, drizzle every one with marinara sauce.
7. After placing the meatballs on the buns, top with mozzarella cheese that has been shredded.
8. Bake under broil for two to three mins, or up to the cheese is bubbling and dilute.
9. Add some fresh basil as a garnish before serving.

Nutrition:

Cals: 400 per serving, Protein: 20g, Carbs: 30g

Fat: 20g, Fiber: 2g

54. Salt and Pepper Crocodile

Prep Time: 15 mins
Cook Time: 10 mins
Total Time: 25 mins
Servings: 4

Ingredients:

- 1 lb crocodile tail fillet, split into strips
- 1/2 cup of cornstarch
- 1 tsp sea salt
- 1 tsp black pepper
- Vegetable oil for frying
- Lemon wedges for serving

Instructions:

1. Mix cornflour, sea salt, and black pepper in a bowl.
2. Make sure the crocodile strips are thoroughly covered by dredging them in the cornflour mixture.

3. In a skillet set over medium-high heat, warm the vegetable oil.
4. Fry the crocodile strips up to they are crispy and golden brown, about two to three mins per side.
5. blot with paper towels.
6. With lemon slices on the side, serve hot.

Nutrition:

Cals: 150 per serving, Protein: 20g, Carbs: 10g

Fat: 5g, Fiber: 1g

55.Tim Tam Chocolate Mousse

Prep Time: 20 mins
Chilling Time: 4 hrs
Total Time: 4 hrs 20 mins
Servings: 6

Ingredients:

- 1 cup of heavy cream
- 200g (7 oz) dark chocolate, chop-up
- 3 Big eggs
- 1/4 cup of granulated sugar
- 1 tsp vanilla extract
- 8 Tim Tam cookies, crushed (+ extra for garnish)

Instructions:

1. Heat the heavy cream in a saucepan up to it starts to simmer.
2. Transfer the chop-up dark chocolate to a heat-resistant bowl and cover it with the heated cream. After a min, give it a quick swirl to make it smooth.
3. Beat the eggs, sugar, and vanilla extract together in a another dish up to they are light and frothy.
4. Whisk continuously as you gradually add the chocolate mixture to the egg mixture.
5. Let the mixture cool up to it reveryes room temperature.
6. Add the crushed Tim Tam cookies and fold gently.
7. After dividing the mousse among serving glasses, chill it for at least four hrs, or up to it solidifies.
8. Before serving, add more crushed Tim Tam cookies as a garnish.
9. Savour the chocolate mousse from Tim Tams!

Nutrition (per serving):

Cals: 350, Protein: 5g, Carbs: 25g, Fat: 25g

Fiber: 2g

56.Grilled Barramundi with Lemon Asparagus

Prep Time: 15 mins
Cook Time: 10 mins

Total Time: 25 mins
Servings: 4

Ingredients:

- 4 barramundi fillets
- 2 bunches asparagus, trimmed
- 2 tbsp olive oil
- 2 cloves garlic, chop-up
- Zest of 1 lemon
- Salt and pepper as needed
- Fresh parsley for garnish
- Lemon wedges for serving

Instructions:

1. Set the grill's temperature to medium-high.
2. Mix asparagus, lemon zest, olive oil, salt, and pepper in a bowl.
3. Barramundi fillets Must be cooked through after grilling for 3–4 mins on every side.
4. Add the asparagus on the grill and cook it for the last few mins of grilling up to it is crisp-tender.
5. Arrange the asparagus and barramundi fillets on a serving plate.
6. Serve with lemon wedges and garnish with fresh parsley.
7. Savour your Lemon Asparagus and Grilled Barramundi!

Nutrition (per serving):

Cals: 300, Protein: 25g, Carbs: 8g, Fat: 18g

Fiber: 4g

57.Vegemite and Cheese Stuffed Bell Peppers

Prep Time: 15 mins
Cook Time: 25 mins
Total Time: 40 mins
Servings: 4

Ingredients:

- 4 bell peppers, halved and seeds take outd
- 1 cup of cooked quinoa
- 1 cup of shredded cheddar cheese
- 1/4 cup of Vegemite
- 1 cup of cherry tomatoes, halved
- Fresh parsley for garnish

Instructions:

1. Preheat the oven to 190°C (375°F).
2. Mix shredded cheddar cheese, cooked quinoa, and Vegemite in a bowl.
3. Stuff the quinoa mixture into every side of a bell pepper.
4. The filled peppers Must be put in a roasting tray.

5. Place half cherry tomatoes on top of every stuffed pepper.
6. Bake the peppers for 25 mins, or up to they are soft.
7. Add fresh parsley as a garnish.
8. Present your cheese-and-vegemite-stuffed bell peppers!

Nutrition (per serving):
Cals: 250, Protein: 10g, Carbs: 25g, Fat: 12g
Fiber: 5g

58. Pepperberry Kangaroo Stir-Fry

Prep Time: 20 mins
Cook Time: 10 mins
Total Time: 30 mins
Servings: 4

Ingredients:

- 1 lb kangaroo meat, thinly split
- 2 tbsp soy sauce
- 1 tbsp oyster sauce
- 1 tbsp hoisin sauce
- 1 tsp pepperberry (or black pepper)
- 2 tbsp vegetable oil
- 1 onion, thinly split
- 1 red bell pepper, thinly split
- 1 green bell pepper, thinly split
- 2 cloves garlic, chop-up
- 1 tbsp fresh ginger, finely grated
- Steamed rice for serving
- Sesame seeds for garnish

Instructions:

1. Marinate the kangaroo meat in a mixture of pepperberry, hoisin sauce, oyster sauce, and soy sauce in a basin. Give it fifteen mins to sit.
2. In a big skillet or wok, heat the vegetable oil over high heat.
3. The marinated kangaroo meat Must be stir-fried up to browned. Remove from the pan and set aside.
4. If necessary, add a little extra oil to the same wok.
5. Green bell pepper, red bell pepper, and onion Must all be stir-fried up to just barely soft.
6. Add the finely grated ginger and chop-up garlic, and stir-fry for an additional min.
7. Place the cooked kangaroo meat back into the wok and mix all the ingredients.
8. Put the stir-fry on top of some steaming rice.
9. Add sesame seeds as a garnish.
10. Savour your Stir-Fried Pepperberry Kangaroo!

Nutrition (per serving):
Cals: 300, Protein: 25g, Carbs: 20g, Fat: 12g
Fiber: 4g

59. Wattleseed Anzac Ice Cream

Prep Time: 20 mins
Churning Time: 30 mins
Freezing Time: 4 hrs
Total Time: 4 hrs 50 mins
Servings: 6

Ingredients:

- 2 cups of heavy cream
- 1 cup of whole milk
- 1 cup of granulated sugar
- 1/2 cup of wattleseed
- 1 tsp vanilla extract
- 1/2 cup of Anzac biscuits, cut up

Instructions:

1. Heat the heavy cream, whole milk, and sugar in a saucepan over medium heat up to the sugar is completely dissolved.
2. After adding the wattleseed, stir and boil the mixture gently.
3. Take it off the stove, cover it and steep it for fifteen mins.
4. Press down on the mixture to extract as much flavour as you can as you strain it to take out the wattleseed.
5. After adding the vanilla essence, stir the mixture and refrigerate it.
6. Following the manufacturer's instructions, churn the mixture in an ice cream machine when it has cooled.
7. Add the cut up Anzac cookies during the last few mins of churning.
8. Once the ice cream is in a container with a lid, freeze it for a minimum of four hrs, or up to it solidifies.
9. Enjoy your Wattleseed Anzac Ice Cream by scooping it up!

Nutrition (per serving):
Cals: 400, Protein: 3g, Carbs: 40g, Fat: 25g
Fiber: 1g

60. Australian Lamb Koftas with Tzatziki

Prep Time: 20 mins
Cook Time: 15 mins
Total Time: 35 mins
Servings: 4

Ingredients:

- For the Lamb Koftas:

- 1 lb ground Australian lamb
- 1/2 cup of breadcrumbs
- 1/4 cup of fresh parsley, chop-up
- 1 tsp ground cumin
- 1 tsp ground coriander
- 1/2 tsp ground cinnamon
- Salt and pepper as needed
- Olive oil for grilling
- For the Tzatziki:
- 1 cup of Greek yogurt
- 1 cucumber, finely grated and drained
- 2 cloves garlic, chop-up
- 1 tbsp fresh dill, chop-up
- 1 tbsp lemon juice
- Salt and pepper as needed

Instructions:

1. To make the Lamb Koftas, put the ground Australian lamb, breadcrumbs, chop-up parsley, powder cinnamon, ground cumin, and ground coriander in a bowl and season with salt and pepper.
2. Blend up to thoroughly blended.
3. Separate the ingredients into equal parts and mould every into a sausage-like shape, called kofta.
4. On a grill or in a grill pan, warm up the olive oil over medium-high heat.
5. Cook, turning regularly, the lamb koftas, on the grill for 5 to 7 mins, or up to cooked through.
6. Take them off the grill and let them to cool.
7. Greek yoghurt, finely grated and drained cucumber, chop-up garlic, chop-up fresh dill, lemon juice, salt, and pepper Must all be mixd in a basin to make tzatziki.
8. Mix thoroughly up to fully incorporated.
9. Present the Lamb Koftas alongside Tzatziki.
10. Place the grilled lamb koftas onto a serving dish.
11. Accompany with the ready-made tzatziki.
12. Savour delicious lamb kebabs from Australia with tzatziki!

Nutrition (per serving):
Cals: 400, Protein: 25g, Carbs: 15g, Fat: 28g
Fiber: 2g

61.Damper Bread Bruschetta

Prep Time: 15 mins
Baking Time: 20 mins
Total Time: 35 mins
Servings: 4

Ingredients:

- For the Damper Bread:

- 2 cups of self-rising flour
- 1/2 tsp salt
- 1 cup of milk
- For the Bruschetta:
- 4 slices damper bread
- 2 tomatoes, diced
- 1/4 cup of red onion, lightly chop-up
- 1/4 cup of fresh basil, chop-up
- 2 tbsp balsamic glaze
- Salt and pepper as needed

Instructions:

1. To make the Damper Bread, preheat the oven to 190°C, or 375°F.
2. Mix salt and self-rising flour in a bowl.
3. Add milk gradually while stirring to produce a soft dough.
4. Place the dough on a surface dusted with flour and gently knead it.
5. Roll out the dough, put it on a baking sheet, and crisscross the top.
6. The damper bread Must be baked for 20 mins, or up to it is golden brown and hollow to the touch.
7. Let it cool down before Cutting.
8. To make the bruschetta, mix the diced tomatoes, fresh basil, red onion, and balsamic glaze in a bowl along with salt and pepper.
9. Toast the slices of damper bread and spread the tomato mixture over them.
10. Present your Bruschetta with Damper Bread!

Nutrition (per serving):
Cals: 300, Protein: 8g, Carbs: 50g, Fat: 6g
Fiber: 3g

62.Macadamia Crusted Barramundi

Prep Time: 15 mins
Cook Time: 15 mins
Total Time: 30 mins
Servings: 4

Ingredients:

- 4 barramundi fillets
- 1 cup of macadamia nuts, lightly chop-up
- 1/2 cup of breadcrumbs
- 1/4 cup of fresh parsley, chop-up
- 2 tbsp Dijon mustard
- 2 tbsp olive oil
- Salt and pepper as needed
- Lemon wedges for serving

Instructions:

1. Set oven temperature to 400°F, or 200°C.

2. Acd the breadcrumbs, chop-up fresh parsley, Di on mustard, olive oil, salt, and pepper to a bowl and mix well.
3. Barramundi fillets Must be patted dry with paper towel.
4. To ensure even coating, press the macadamia mixture onto every fillet.
5. Arrange the fillets onto a parchment paper-lined baking sheet.
6. Bake the barramundi for 12 to 15 mins, or up to the crust is brown and the fish is cooked through.
7. Accompany with wedges of lemon.
8. Savour your Barramundi with Macadamia Crusted!

Nutrition (per serving):

Cals: 350, Protein: 30g, Carbs: 10g, Fat: 22g
Fiber: 3g

63.Vegemite and Cheese Savory Muffins

Prep Time: 15 mins
Cook Time: 20 mins
Total Time: 35 mins
Servings: 12

Ingredients:

- 2 cups of all-purpose flour
- 1 tbsp baking powder
- 1/2 tsp baking soda
- 1/4 tsp salt
- 1/4 cup of unsalted butter, dilute
- 1/4 cup of Vegemite
- 1 cup of milk
- 1 egg
- 1 cup of shredded cheese (cheddar or your choice)
- Chop-up fresh parsley for garnish

Instructions:

1. Heat the oven to 375°F (190°C) and place paper liners into a muffin tray.
2. Mix the flour, baking soda, baking powder, and salt in a big bowl.
3. Mix the egg, milk, Vegemite, and dilute butter in a another bowl.
4. Mixing up to just combined, pour the wet components into the dry ingredients.
5. Add the cheese shreds and fold.
6. Pour the batter into every muffin cup of, filling it to approximately two thirds of the way.
7. When a toothpick inserted into the centre comes out clean, bake for 18 to 20 mins.
8. After a few mins, let the muffins cool before moving them to a wire rack.

9. Before serving, sprinkle some freshly chop-up parsley on top.

Nutrition:

Cals: 150 per muffin, Protein: 5g, Carbs: 15g, Fat: 8g, Fiber: 1g

64.Salt and Pepper Prawn Pizza

Prep Time: 15 mins
Cook Time: 15 mins
Total Time: 30 mins
Servings: 4

Ingredients:

- 1 pizza dough, homemade or store-bought
- 1/2 cup of pizza sauce
- 1 cup of shredded mozzarella cheese
- 1/2 lb prawns, peel off and deveined
- 2 tbsp olive oil
- 1 tsp sea salt
- 1 tsp black pepper
- Fresh cilantro for garnish
- Lemon wedges for serving

Instructions:

1. Set the oven to the temperature recommended by the box/pkg of pizza dough or by using a handmade recipe.
2. Using a floured surface, roll out the pizza dough and place it on a baking sheet or pizza stone.
3. Leaving a space for the crust, cover the dough with pizza sauce.
4. Evenly scatter mozzarella cheese shreds on top of the sauce.
5. Toss prawns with olive oil, black pepper, and sea salt in a bowl.
6. Place the spiced prawns in a row on the pie.
7. Bake the dough as directed on the dough, or up to the cheese has dilute and the crust is brown.
8. Add some fresh cilantro as a garnish and serve with wedges of lemon on the side.

Nutrition:

Cals: 300 per serving, Protein: 15g, Carbs: 30g
Fat: 15g, Fiber: 2g

65.Tim Tam Slam Milkshake

Prep Time: 5 mins
Cook Time: 0 mins
Total Time: 5 mins
Servings: 2

Ingredients:

- 4 cups of vanilla ice cream

- 1 cup of milk
- 4 Tim Tam biscuits
- Whipped cream for topping
- Crushed Tim Tam biscuits for garnish

Instructions:

1. Blend together milk, Tim Tam biscuits, and vanilla ice cream using a blender. Process till smooth.
2. Fill glasses with the milkshake.
3. Add some crushed Tim Tam biscuits and whipped cream on top.
4. Savour your Tim Tam Slam Milkshake right away!

Nutrition:

Cals: 400 per serving, Protein: 8g, Carbs: 40g

Fat: 22g, Fiber: 1g

66.Kangaroo and Mushroom Risotto

Prep Time: 10 mins
Cook Time: 30 mins
Total Time: 40 mins
Servings: 4

Ingredients:

- 1 lb kangaroo meat, diced
- 1 cup of Arborio rice
- 1/2 cup of dry white wine
- 4 cups of beef or vegetable broth, kept warm
- 1 onion, lightly chop-up
- 2 cloves garlic, chop-up
- 1 cup of mushrooms, split
- finely grated Parmesan cheese, half a cup
- 2 tbsp butter
- Salt and pepper as needed
- Fresh parsley for garnish

Instructions:

1. Heat the olive oil in a big skillet over medium-high heat.
2. Cook chop-up kangaroo meat till it turns brown. Remove from the pan and set aside.
3. Chop-up garlic and chop-up onion Must be cooked in the same skillet up to they become soft.
4. After adding the mushrooms, simmer for an additional two to three mins.
5. Add the Arborio rice and let it cook for a further two mins.
6. Add the dry white wine and whisk up to it is absorbed.
7. One ladle of warm broth at a time, add and stir up to absorbed before adding another ladle.
8. This process Must be repeated up to the rice is cooked through and creamy.

9. Add butter, finely grated Parmesan cheese, and cooked kangaroo meat. Add pepper and salt for seasoning.
10. Before serving, garnish with fresh parsley.

Nutrition:

Cals: 400 per serving, Protein: 20g, Carbs: 40g

Fat: 15g, Fiber: 2g

67.Anzac Biscuit Pancakes

Prep Time: 10 mins
Cook Time: 15 mins
Total Time: 25 mins
Servings: 4

Ingredients:

- 1 cup of all-purpose flour
- 2 tbsp sugar
- 1 tsp baking powder
- 1/2 tsp baking soda
- 1/4 tsp salt
- 1 cup of buttermilk
- 1 Big egg
- 2 tbsp dilute butter
- 1/2 cup of rolled oats
- 1/4 cup of shredded coconut
- 1/4 cup of golden syrup
- Butter or oil for cooking
- Maple syrup for serving

Instructions:

1. Mix the flour, sugar, baking soda, baking powder, and salt in a big bowl.
2. Beat the egg, dilute butter, and buttermilk together in a another basin.
3. Mixing up to just combined, pour the wet components into the dry ingredients.
4. Stir in golden syrup, shredded coconut, and rolled oats.
5. Grease a skillet or griddle with butter or oil and heat it over medium heat.
6. Spoon quarter-cup of measures of batter onto the griddle and cook up to bubbles appear on top.
7. When the other side is golden brown, flip and continue cooking.
8. Proceed with the leftover batter.
9. Drizzle some maple syrup over the steaming pancakes and serve.

Nutrition:

Cals: 300 per serving, Protein: 6g, Carbs: 40g

Fat: 12g, Fiber: 2g

68. Australian Beef Pie with Mushy Peas

Prep Time: 20 mins
Cook Time: 40 mins
Total Time: 1 hr
Servings: 4

Ingredients:

- 1 lb ground beef
- 1 onion, chop-up
- 2 carrots, diced
- 2 cloves garlic, chop-up
- 2 tbsp tomato paste
- 1 cup of beef broth
- 1 tsp Worcestershire sauce
- 1 tsp dried thyme
- Salt and pepper as needed
- 1 cup of refrigerate peas
- 1 box/pkg (17.3 oz) puff pastry, thawed
- 1 egg, beaten

Instructions:

1. Set oven temperature to 400°F, or 200°C.
2. Brown the ground beef over medium-high heat in a Big skillet.
3. Add the chop-up garlic, diced carrots, and chop-up onion. Toss the vegetables in a skillet and cook until they are soft.
4. Add the dried thyme, Worcestershire sauce, beef stock, tomato paste, salt, and pepper. Simmer for ten to fifteen mins.
5. Cook for a further five mins after adding the refrigerate peas.
6. On a surface dusted with flour, roll out the puff pastry.
7. Slice out circles that will fit the tops of a big baking dish or individual pie pans.
8. Filling dishes with beef mixture spooned into them.
9. Place rounds of puff pastry on top and press down the corners to seal.
10. Spread some beaten egg over the pastry.
11. Bake for twenty to twenty-five mins, or up to the pastry is cooked through and golden brown.
12. Alongside the meat pies, serve mushy peas.

Nutrition:

Cals: 500 per serving, Protein: 25g, Carbs: 40g
Fat: 30g, Fiber: 3g

69. Barramundi Burgers with Mango Salsa

Prep Time: 15 mins
Cook Time: 10 mins
Total Time: 25 mins
Servings: 4

Ingredients:

- 1 lb barramundi fillets
- 1 tbsp olive oil
- 1 tsp cumin
- 1 tsp paprika
- Salt and pepper as needed
- 4 burger buns
- Lettuce leaves for serving
- Mango Salsa:
- 1 ripe mango, diced
- 1/2 red onion, lightly chop-up
- 1/4 cup of fresh cilantro, chop-up
- Juice of 1 lime
- Salt and pepper as needed

Instructions:

1. Set a grill pan or the grill to medium-high heat.
2. Marinate barramundi fillets in olive oil, salt, pepper, cumin, and paprika.
3. Barramundi fillets Must be cooked through after grilling for 3–4 mins on every side.
4. To make the salsa, place the chop-up red onion, chop-up cilantro, split mango, lime juice, salt, and pepper in a bowl.
5. On the grill, toast the hamburger buns.
6. Place the barramundi fillets on the buns, then top with the lettuce leaves and mango salsa to assemble the burgers.
7. Enjoy while hot!

Nutrition:

Cals: 350 per serving, Protein: 20g, Carbs: 40g, Fat: 12g, Fiber: 3g

70. Vegemite and Cheese Stuffed Jalapeños

Prep Time: 15 mins
Cook Time: 15 mins
Total Time: 30 mins
Servings: 8

Ingredients:

- 16 fresh jalapeños
- 8 oz cream cheese, melted
- 1/4 cup of Vegemite
- 1 cup of shredded cheese (cheddar or your choice)
- 1/2 cup of breadcrumbs
- Olive oil for brushing

Instructions:

1. Before proceeding, preheat the oven to 375°F (190°C) and place parchment paper on a baking pan.
2. Slice jalapeños lengthwise, then take out the seeds and membranes.

3. Blend melted cream cheese and Vegemite together in a bowl.
4. In every half of a jalapeño, stuff the cream cheese mixture.
5. Over the packed jalapeños, scatter some shredded cheese.
6. Dust the packed jalapeños with breadcrumbs in a different bowl.
7. Put the filled jalapeños onto the baking sheet that has been ready.
8. Drizzle some olive oil over the tops.
9. Bake for fifteen mins, or up to the cheese is bubbling and dilute and the jalapeños are soft.
10. Enjoy while hot!

Nutrition:

Cals: 200 per serving, Protein: 8g, Carbs: 10g

Fat: 15g, Fiber: 2g

71. Chicken and Leek Damper Pie

Prep Time: 20 mins
Cook Time: 30 mins
Total Time: 50 mins
Servings: 6

Ingredients:

- For the Filling:
- 2 cups of cooked chicken, shredded
- 1 leek, thinly split
- 1 cup of refrigerate peas
- 1 cup of chicken broth
- 1/2 cup of heavy cream
- 2 tbsp all-purpose flour
- 2 tbsp butter
- Salt and pepper as needed
- For the Damper Crust:
- 2 cups of self-rising flour
- 1/2 tsp salt
- 1 cup of milk

Instructions:

1. Melt butter in a pot over medium heat for the filling.
2. Cook the split leek up to it becomes tender.
3. Add the flour and cook for one to two mins.
4. Add the heavy cream and chicken broth gradually and whisk up to smooth.
5. Add refrigerate peas and shredded chicken. Cook up to well heated.
6. As needed, add salt and pepper for seasoning.
7. For the Crust of Dampers:
8. Set oven temperature to 400°F, or 200°C.
9. Mix salt and self-rising flour in a bowl.

10. Add milk gradually while stirring to produce a soft dough.
11. Place the dough on a surface dusted with flour and gently knead it.
12. Roll out the dough to the pie dish's dimensions.
13. Fill the pie plate with the chicken and leek filling.
14. Sealed around the edges, cover with the damper crust.
15. Bake the crust for 25 to 30 mins, or up to it turns golden brown.
16. Before serving, let it to cool slightly.
17. Savour the delicious Leek and Chicken Damper Pie!

Nutrition (per serving):

Cals: 400, Protein: 20g, Carbs: 35g, Fat: 18g

Fiber: 3g

72. Quandong Glazed Lamb Chops

Prep Time: 15 mins
Marinating Time: 2 hrs
Cook Time: 15 mins
Total Time: 2 hrs 30 mins
Servings: 4

Ingredients:

- 8 lamb chops
- 1/2 cup of quandong (wild pevery) jam
- 2 tbsp soy sauce
- 2 tbsp olive oil
- 2 cloves garlic, chop-up
- 1 tsp dried rosemary
- Salt and pepper as needed
- Fresh parsley for garnish

Instructions:

1. Mix quandong jam, dried rosemary, olive oil, soy sauce, chop-up garlic, and salt and pepper in a bowl.
2. Pour the marinade over the lamb chops and place them in a shlet dish.
3. For the flavours to fully integrate, cover and chill for a minimum of two hrs.
4. Turn the heat up to medium-high on the grill or grill pan.
5. Lamb chops Must be cooked to your preference after grilling for 5 to 7 mins on every side.
6. While grilling, baste with the leftover marinade.
7. Before serving, garnish with fresh parsley.
8. Savour your Lamb Chops with Quandong Glaze!

Nutrition (per serving):

Cals: 450, Protein: 30g, Carbs: 15g, Fat: 30g

Fiber: 2g

73.Wattleseed Anzac Popsicles

Prep Time: 15 mins
Freezing Time: 6 hrs
Total Time: 6 hrs 15 mins
Servings: 6

Ingredients:

- 1 cup of rolled oats
- 1 cup of shredded coconut
- 1 cup of almond milk
- 1/2 cup of wattleseed
- 1/2 cup of honey
- 1/2 cup of Greek yogurt
- 1/2 cup of chop-up Anzac biscuits

Instructions:

1. Blend together rolled oats, Greek yoghurt, shredded coconut, almond milk, wattleseed, and honey in a blender. Process till smooth.
2. Acd chop-up Anzac biscuits and stir.
3. Transfer the blend into popsicle moulds.
4. Place the popsicle sticks in and freeze up to solid, about 6 hrs.
5. After removing from the moulds, savour your Wattleseed Anzac Pops!

Nutrition (per serving):

Cals: 200, Protein: 5g, Carbs: 25g, Fat: 10g
Fiber: 3g

74.Aussie Meatball Spaghetti

Prep Time: 30 mins
Cook Time: 25 mins
Total Time: 55 mins
Servings: 4

Ingredients:

- For the Meatballs:
- 1 lb ground beef
- 1/2 cup of breadcrumbs
- Finely shredded Parmesan cheese, 1/4 cup
- 1 egg
- 2 cloves garlic, chop-up
- 1 tsp dried oregano
- Salt and pepper as needed
- For the Tomato Sauce:
- 1 can (28 oz) crushed tomatoes
- 1 onion, lightly chop-up
- 2 cloves garlic, chop-up
- 2 tbsp tomato paste
- 1 tsp dried basil
- 1 tsp dried oregano
- Salt and pepper as needed
- Other:

- 8 oz spaghetti
- Fresh basil for garnish
- Finely grated Parmesan cheese for serving

Instructions:

1. Set the oven's temperature to 375°F (190°C) for the meatballs.
2. Ground beef, breadcrumbs, egg, finely grated Parmesan cheese, chop-up garlic, dried oregano, salt, and pepper Must all be mixd in a bowl.
3. Put the mixture on a baking sheet and form it into meatballs.
4. Bake for 20 to 25 mins, or up to thoroughly done.
5. Regarding the Tomato Sauce:
6. Chop the onion and sauté it in a saucepan up to it gets tender.
7. Add the chop-up garlic and continue cooking for one more min.
8. Add salt, pepper, dried oregano, dried basil, smashed tomatoes, and tomato paste.
9. Give the sauce a 15 to 20-min simmer.
10. Regarding the spaghetti: Prepare the spaghetti per the directions on the box/pkg.
11. Mix the tomato sauce with the cooked spaghetti.
12. Place meatballs over the spaghetti to serve.
13. Add finely grated Parmesan cheese and fresh basil as garnish.
14. Savour the Australian Meatball Spaghetti!

Nutrition (per serving):

Cals: 500, Protein: 25g, Carbs: 40g, Fat: 25g
Fiber: 5g

75.Kangaroo Kofta Skewers

Prep Time: 20 mins
Marinating Time: 1 hr
Cook Time: 10 mins
Total Time: 1 hr 30 mins
Servings: 4

Ingredients:

- For the Kofta:
- 1 lb ground kangaroo meat
- 1 onion, finely grated
- 2 cloves garlic, chop-up
- 1 tsp ground cumin
- 1 tsp ground coriander
- 1/2 tsp smoked paprika
- Salt and pepper as needed
- For the Yogurt Sauce:
- 1 cup of Greek yogurt
- 1 cucumber, finely grated and drained
- 2 tbsp fresh mint, chop-up
- 1 tbsp lemon juice

- Salt and pepper as needed
- Other:
- Skewers, soaked in water

Instructions:

1. To make the Kofta, mix together ground kangaroo meat, smoked paprika, chop-up garlic, shredded onion, ground cumin, and ground coriander in a bowl with salt and pepper.
2. Blend up to thoroughly blended.
3. After dividing the mixture, form it onto skewers.
4. Let it marinate for a minimum of 60 mins in the fridge.
5. In a bowl, mix Greek yoghurt, finely grated and drained cucumber, chop-up fresh mint, lemon juice, salt, and pepper to make the yoghurt sauce.
6. Mix thoroughly up to fully incorporated.
7. Set the grill's temperature to medium-high before grilling.
8. The kofta skewers Must be cooked through after grilling for 4–5 mins on every side.
9. Present the yoghurt sauce alongside.
10. Savour your kangaroo kebabs using skewers.

Nutrition (per serving):
Cals: 350, Protein: 20g, Carbs: 15g, Fat: 25g
Fiber: 2g

76.Lemon Myrtle Grilled Chicken Wings

Prep Time: 10 mins
Marinating Time: 2 hrs
Cook Time: 20 mins
Total Time: 2 hrs 30 mins
Servings: 4

Ingredients:

- 2 lbs chicken wings
- 1/4 cup of olive oil
- Zest and juice of 2 lemons
- 2 tbsp honey
- 2 tsp dried lemon myrtle
- 2 cloves garlic, chop-up
- Salt and pepper as needed
- Fresh lemon wedges for serving

Instructions:

1. Olive oil, zest, juice, honey, dried lemon myrtle, chop-up garlic, salt, and pepper Must all be mixd in a basin.
2. Pour the marinade over the chicken wings and place them in a plastic bag that can be sealed.
3. To let the flavours to infuse, seal the bag and place it in the refrigerator for at least two hrs.
4. Set the grill's temperature to medium-high.

5. The chicken wings Must be cooked through and golden after 18 to 20 mins on the grill, turning them over once.
6. Accompany with wedges of fresh lemon.
7. Savour your Grilled Chicken Wings with Lemon Myrtle!

Nutrition (per serving):
Cals: 400, Protein: 25g, Carbs: 10g, Fat: 30g
Fiber: 1g

77.Macadamia Nut Hummus

Prep Time: 10 mins
Total Time: 10 mins
Servings: 8

Ingredients:

- 1 can (15 oz) chickpeas, drained and rinsed
- 1/2 cup of macadamia nuts
- 1/4 cup of tahini
- 2 cloves garlic, chop-up
- Juice of 1 lemon
- 1/4 cup of olive oil
- Salt and pepper as needed
- Paprika and chop-up parsley for garnish

Instructions:

1. Chickpeas, macadamia nuts, tahini, chop-up garlic, and lemon juice Must all be mixd in a mixer.
2. Process till everything is smooth.
3. Olive oil Must be added gradually while the machine is operating, up to the hummus has the consistency you want.
4. As needed, add salt and pepper for seasoning.
5. Move the hummus into a bowl for serving.
6. Add some chop-up parsley and paprika as garnish.
7. With your preferred dippers, serve your Macadamia Nut Hummus.
8. Have fun!

Nutrition (per serving):
Cals: 200, Protein: 5g, Carbs: 10g, Fat: 15g
Fiber: 3g

78.Barramundi with Lemon Myrtle Gremolata

Prep Time: 15 mins
Cook Time: 15 mins
Total Time: 30 mins
Servings: 4

Ingredients:

- For the Barramundi:
- 4 barramundi fillets
- 2 tbsp olive oil
- Salt and pepper as needed
- For the Lemon Myrtle Gremolata:
- Zest of 2 lemons
- 2 tbsp fresh parsley, chop-up
- 2 tbsp fresh lemon juice
- 2 tbsp olive oil
- Salt and pepper as needed

Instructions:

1. Regarding the Barramundi:
2. Set oven temperature to 400°F, or 200°C.
3. After patting dry, season barramundi fillets with salt and pepper.
4. In a skillet that is ovensafe, warm the olive oil over medium-high heat.
5. Marinate barramundi fillets for two to three mins on every side.
6. After transferring the skillet to the preheated oven, bake the barramundi for a further 8 to 10 mins, or up to it is thoroughly cooked.
7. For the Gremolata with Lemon Myrtle:
8. Mix lemon zest, fresh parsley that has been slice, lemon juice, olive oil, salt, and pepper in a bowl.
9. Over the fried barramundi fillets, spoon the gremolata.
10. Arrange some Lemon Myrtle Gremolata alongside your barramundi!

Nutrition (per serving):

Cals: 300, Protein: 30g, Carbs: 2g, Fat: 20g

Fiber: 1g

79.Vegemite and Cheese Stuffed Pretzels

Prep Time: 30 mins
Resting Time: 1 hr
Cook Time: 15 mins
Total Time: 1 hr 45 mins
Servings: 8

Ingredients:

- For the Pretzel Dough:
- 1 1/2 cups of warm water
- 1 tbsp sugar
- 2 tsp salt
- 4 cups of all-purpose flour
- 2 1/4 tsp active dry yeast
- 1/4 cup of unsalted butter, dilute
- For the Filling:
- 1/2 cup of Vegemite

- 1 1/2 cups of shredded cheese (cheddar or your choice)
- For Boiling:
- 10 cups of water
- 2/3 cup of baking soda
- For Topping:
- Flaky sea salt

Instructions:

1. To make the pretzel dough, mix sugar, salt, and warm water in a bowl. After adding the yeast, cover the liquid and leave for five mins.
2. To the yeast mixture, add the flour and the dilute butter. Work the dough up to it comes together.
3. On a surface dusted with flour, knead the dough up to smooth.
4. After adding oil to a bowl, cover it, and let the dough rise for an hr.
5. Roll out the dough to create a Big rectangle for the filling.
6. Evenly distribute Vegemite over the dough.
7. Over the Vegemite, scatter the shredded cheese.
8. To assemble, roll the dough tightly starting from the long side and shape it into a log.
9. Slice the timber into eight equal pieces.
10. Turn the oven on to 450°F, or 230°C.
11. Bring ten cups of water and baking soda to a boil in a big pot.
12. After 30 seconds of boiling, lay every pretzel on a baking sheet covered with parchment paper.
13. To bake, lightly dust pretzels with flakes of sea salt.
14. Bake for 12 to 15 mins, up to the colour turns golden.
15. To serve, let them cool somewhat.
16. Savour the Cheese and Vegemite Stuffed Pretzels!

Nutrition (per serving):

Cals: 350, Protein: 10g, Carbs: 50g, Fat: 12g

Fiber: 3g

80.Salt and Pepper Prawn Stir-Fry

Prep Time: 15 mins
Cook Time: 10 mins
Total Time: 25 mins
Servings: 4

Ingredients:

- 1 lb Big prawns, peel off and deveined
- 2 tbsp cornstarch
- 2 tbsp vegetable oil
- 4 cloves garlic, chop-up
- 1 tbsp fresh ginger, finely grated

- 2 red chili peppers, split
- 1 bell pepper, thinly split
- 1 cup of snap peas
- 2 tbsp soy sauce
- 1 tbsp oyster sauce
- 1 tsp black pepper
- 1 green onion, chop-up
- Sesame seeds for garnish

Instructions:

1. Once coated, toss the prawns in cornflour.
2. In a big skillet or wok, heat the vegetable oil over high heat.
3. Add the chop-up red chilli peppers, finely grated ginger, and chop-up garlic. Stir-fry for a full min.
4. Stir-fry the prawns up to they take on a pink hue.
5. Add the snap peas and bell pepper. finish frying for another two or three minutes.
6. Add the oyster sauce, black pepper, and soy sauce. Mix everything together.
7. Add sesame seeds and split green onions as garnish.
8. Present your salt-and-pepper prawns. Stir-fry with noodles or rice.
9. Have fun!

Nutrition (per serving):
Cals: 250, Protein: 20g, Carbs: 15g, Fat: 12g
Fiber: 3g

81.Tim Tam Milkshake Smoothie Bowl

Prep Time: 10 mins
Total Time: 10 mins
Servings: 2

Ingredients:

- 4 Tim Tam cookies
- 2 cups of vanilla ice cream
- 1 cup of milk
- 1 banana, refrigerate
- 2 tbsp chocolate syrup
- Whipped cream for topping
- Crushed Tim Tam for garnish

Instructions:

1. Blend together milk, refrigerate banana, chocolate syrup, vanilla ice cream, and Tim Tam cookies in a blender.
2. Blend till creamy and smooth.
3. Transfer the smoothie to bowls.
4. Add cut up Tim Tams and whipped cream on top.
5. Savour your Smoothie Bowl with Tim Tam Milkshake!

Nutrition (per serving):
Cals: 500, Protein: 8g, Carbs: 60g, Fat: 25g
Fiber: 4g

82.Kangaroo and Quinoa Stuffed Capsicums

Prep Time: 20 mins
Cook Time: 25 mins
Total Time: 45 mins
Servings: 4

Ingredients:

- 4 Big capsicums (bell peppers), halved and seeds take outd
- 1 cup of quinoa, cooked
- 1 lb ground kangaroo meat
- 1 onion, lightly chop-up
- 2 cloves garlic, chop-up
- 1 cup of cherry tomatoes, halved
- 1 cup of rinsed and drained black beans
- 1 tsp ground cumin
- 1 tsp smoked paprika
- Salt and pepper as needed
- 1 cup of shredded cheese (cheddar or your choice)
- Fresh parsley for garnish

Instructions:

1. Preheat the oven to 190°C (375°F).
2. Half the capsicums and put them in a roasting dish.
3. Regarding the Filling:
4. Cook the ground kangaroo meat till browned in a pan.
5. Add chop-up garlic and diced onion. Simmer up to tender.
6. Add the quinoa that has been cooked, cherry tomatoes, black beans, smoked paprika, ground cumin, and salt and pepper.
7. Fill the half-capsicums with a spoonful of filling.
8. To bake, place shredded cheese on top of every stuffed bell pepper.
9. Bake for twenty-five mins, or up to the cheese has dilute and the capsicums are soft.
10. Add fresh parsley as a garnish.
11. Present your Quinoa and Kangaroo Stuffed Capsules!

Nutrition (per serving):
Cals: 400, Protein: 25g, Carbs: 40g, Fat: 15g
Fiber: 8g

83.Wattleseed Anzac Trifle

Prep Time: 20 mins
Total Time: 20 mins
Servings: 8

Ingredients:

- 1 batch of Anzac biscuits, cut up
- 2 cups of vanilla custard
- 2 cups of whipped cream
- 1 cup of Wattleseed-infused caramel sauce (or regular caramel sauce)
- 1 cup of shredded coconut, toasted
- Fresh berries for garnish

Instructions:

1. Cut up the Anzac biscuits and place them in the bottom of a trifle dish or individual glasses.
2. Regarding Layering:
3. Cover the biscuits with half of the caramel sauce flavoured with wattleseed.
4. Over the caramel layer, distribute half of the vanilla custard.
5. Spread some whipped cream on top.
6. Add half of the shredded coconut that has been roasted.
7. Iterate the Layers:
8. cut up biscuits for Anzac
9. Any leftover caramel sauce
10. The leftover vanilla custard
11. Remaining whipped cream
12. The remaining coconut shreds, roasted
13. Top with some fresh berries as a garnish.
14. Keep chilled up to you're ready to serve.
15. Enjoy your Anzac Trifle, Wattleseed!

Nutrition (per serving):

Cals: 350, Protein: 5g, Carbs: 45g, Fat: 18g
Fiber: 3g

84.Aussie Meatball Sliders

Prep Time: 20 mins
Cook Time: 20 mins
Total Time: 40 mins
Servings: 8 sliders

Ingredients:

- For the Meatballs:
- 1 lb ground beef
- 1/2 cup of breadcrumbs
- Finely shredded Parmesan cheese, 1/4 cup
- 1 egg
- 2 cloves garlic, chop-up
- 1 tsp dried oregano
- Salt and pepper as needed
- For the Tomato Sauce:
- 1 can (14 oz) crushed tomatoes

- 1 onion, lightly chop-up
- 2 cloves garlic, chop-up
- 1 tsp dried basil
- 1 tsp dried oregano
- Salt and pepper as needed
- Other:
- 8 slider buns
- 1 cup of shredded mozzarella cheese
- Fresh basil for garnish

Instructions:

1. Set the oven's temperature to 375°F (190°C) for the meatballs.
2. Ground beef, breadcrumbs, egg, finely grated Parmesan cheese, chop-up garlic, dried oregano, salt, and pepper Must all be mixd in a bowl.
3. Put the mixture on a baking sheet and form it into tiny meatballs.
4. Bake for 15 to 20 mins, or up to thoroughly done.
5. Regarding the Tomato Sauce:
6. Chop the onion and sauté it in a saucepan up to it gets tender.
7. Add the chop-up garlic and continue cooking for one more min.
8. Add the dried oregano, dry basil, dried tomatoes, salt, and pepper and stir.
9. Cook the sauce for ten to fifteen mins.
10. For Putting Together:
11. After slicing the slider buns, top every bottom half with a meatball.
12. Drizzle every meatball with some tomato sauce.
13. Top with mozzarella cheese that has been shredded.
14. The cheese Must be bubbling and dilute after two to three mins under the grill.
15. Throw some fresh basil on top.
16. Position the upper portion of the slider bun.
17. Savour the Australian Meatball Sliders!

Nutrition (per slider):

Cals: 250, Protein: 15g, Carbs: 20g, Fat: 12g
Fiber: 2g

85.Barramundi with Bush Tomato Butter Sauce

Prep Time: 10 mins
Cook Time: 15 mins
Total Time: 25 mins
Servings: 4

Ingredients:

- For the Barramundi:
- 4 barramundi fillets
- Salt and pepper as needed

- 2 tbsp olive oil
- For the Bush Tomato Butter Sauce:
- 1/2 cup of unsalted butter
- 2 tbsp bush tomato chutney
- 1 tbsp lemon juice
- 1 tsp dried thyme
- Salt and pepper as needed

Instructions:

1. To prepare the barramundi, sprinkle some salt and pepper on the fillets.
2. In a skillet set over medium-high heat, warm the olive oil.
3. Barramundi fillets Must be seared for 3–4 mins on every side, or up to done.
4. Regarding the Butter Sauced Bush Tomato:
5. Melt unsalted butter in a pot over a medium heat.
6. Add the lemon juice, dried thyme, bush tomato chutney, salt, and pepper and stir.
7. Let the flavours to mingle by cooking for two to three mins.
8. Arrange the barramundi fillets on plates for serving.
9. Drizzle with the buttery bush tomato sauce.
10. Savour your barramundi with butter sauce made from Bush tomatoes!

Nutrition (per serving):
Cals: 350, Protein: 25g, Carbs: 2g, Fat: 28g
Fiber: 1g

86.Barramundi with Bush Tomato Pesto

Prep Time: 15 mins
Cook Time: 15 mins
Total Time: 30 mins
Servings: 4

Ingredients:

- 4 barramundi fillets
- 1 cup of fresh basil leaves
- 1/2 cup of bush tomatoes, rehydrated
- 1/4 cup of pine nuts, toasted
- finely grated Parmesan cheese, half a cup
- 2 cloves garlic, chop-up
- 1/2 cup of extra-virgin olive oil
- Salt and pepper as needed
- Lemon wedges for serving

Instructions:

1. Add the basil, rehydrated bush tomatoes, roasted pine nuts, finely grated Parmesan, and chop-up garlic to a mixer.
2. Pulse up to chop-up lightly.

3. Olive oil Must be added gradually while the machine is operating, up to the pesto has a smooth consistency.
4. As needed, add salt and pepper for seasoning.
5. Set a grill pan or the grill to medium-high heat.
6. Rub some salt and pepper on the barramundi fillets.
7. Barramundi fillets Must be cooked through after grilling for 3–4 mins on every side.
8. Present barramundi fillets alongside lemon wedges and a generous portion of bush tomato pesto.

Nutrition:
Cals: 350 per serving, Protein: 25g, Carbs: 3g, Fat: 28g
Fiber: 2g

87.Vegemite and Cheese Toastie

Prep Time: 5 mins
Cook Time: 5 mins
Total Time: 10 mins
Servings: 2

Ingredients:

- 4 slices of bread
- Butter, melted
- Vegemite
- 1 cup of shredded cheese (cheddar or your choice)

Instructions:

1. Heat up a pan or sandwich press to a medium temperature.
2. Put a mini amount of butter on one side of every slice of bread.
3. Spread plenty of Vegemite on the sides of two slices that haven't been buttered.
4. Evenly scatter the shredded cheese on top of the Vegemite.
5. Place the remaining bread slices on top, buttered side out.
6. After the bread is golden brown and the cheese has dilute, place the sandwiches in the pan or sandwich press.
7. Turn the sandwiches over carefully and cook the other side.
8. Take out from the flame as soon as the cheese has dilute and both sides are browned.
9. Let cool for one min, then slice into slices and serve.

Nutrition:
Cals: 300 per serving, Protein: 12g, Carbs: 30g
Fat: 15g, Fiber: 2g

88. Salt and Pepper Crocodile Tacos

Prep Time: 20 mins
Cook Time: 10 mins
Total Time: 30 mins
Servings: 4

Ingredients:

- 1 lb crocodile tail fillet, split into strips
- 1/2 cup of all-purpose flour
- 1 tsp sea salt
- 1 tsp black pepper
- 1 tsp garlic powder
- Vegetable oil for frying
- 8 mini flour tortillas
- Shredded lettuce
- Diced tomatoes
- Split red onions
- Sour cream
- Fresh cilantro for garnish
- Lime wedges for serving

Instructions:

1. Mix the flour, black pepper, garlic powder, and sea salt in a bowl.
2. Shake off any excess flour mixture after dredging the crocodile strips in it.
3. The vegetable oil should be heated in a skillet over medium-high heat.
4. Fry the crocodile strips up to they are crispy and golden brown, about two to three mins per side.
5. Blot with paper towels.
6. Use the microwave or a skillet to reheat tortillas.
7. Top every tortilla with a strip of crocodile to assemble the tacos.
8. Add split red onions, diced tomatoes, shredded lettuce, and a dollop of sour cream on top.
9. Serve with lime wedges on the side and garnish with fresh cilantro.

Nutrition:

Cals: 350 per serving, Protein: 25g, Carbs: 35g
Fat: 12g, Fiber: 3g

89. Tim Tam Ice Cream Sandwiches

Prep Time: 10 mins
Cook Time: 0 mins
Total Time: 10 mins
Servings: 4

Ingredients:

- 8 Tim Tam biscuits
- 2 cups of vanilla ice cream, melted
- Crushed Tim Tam biscuits for rolling

Instructions:

1. Line a tray with parchment paper.
2. On one side of a Tim Tam biscuit, generously spread melted vanilla ice cream.
3. To make a sandwich, place another Tim Tam biscuit on top.
4. Coat the ice cream sandwich's edges by rolling them in crushed Tim Tam biscuits.
5. After the tray is ready, arrange the ice cream sandwiches on it.
6. Proceed with the remaining Tim Tam biscuits in the same manner.
7. Once the ice cream is solid, freeze the ice cream sandwiches for a minimum of one to two hrs.
8. Enjoy your Tim Tam Ice Cream Sandwiches after serving!

Nutrition:

Cals: 300 per serving, Protein: 5g, Carbs: 40g
Fat: 15g, Fiber: 1g

90. Bush Tomato Kangaroo Stew

Prep Time: 20 mins
Cook Time: 2 hrs
Total Time: 2 hrs and 20 mins
Servings: 6

Ingredients:

- 1 lb kangaroo stew meat
- 2 tbsp olive oil
- 1 onion, chop-up
- 2 carrots, split
- 2 celery stalks, chop-up
- 3 cloves garlic, chop-up
- 2 tbsp tomato paste
- 1/2 cup of red wine
- 4 cups of beef broth
- 2 cups of diced tomatoes
- 1/4 cup of bush tomatoes, rehydrated
- 1 tsp dried thyme
- 1 bay leaf
- Salt and pepper as needed
- Fresh parsley for garnish

Instructions:

1. Warm up the olive oil in a big pot over medium-high heat.
2. On all sides, brown the meat for kangaroo stew. Take out and place aside.
3. Chop the celery, carrots, and onion and sauté them in the same saucepan up to they are soft.
4. Stir for one to two mins after adding the tomato paste and chop-up garlic.

5. To deglaze the pot and scrape away any browned bits, pour in some red wine.
6. Back in the pot, add the browned kangaroo meat.
7. Add the dried thyme, bay leaf, diced tomatoes, rehydrated bush tomatoes, salt, and pepper along with the beef broth.
8. Once the kangaroo meat is tender, simmer the stew for two hrs on low heat after bringing it to a boil.
9. Before serving, take the bay leaf off.
10. Add some fresh parsley as a garnish and serve the hot bush tomato kangaroo stew.

Nutrition:
Cals: 300 per serving, Protein: 25g, Carbs: 15g
Fat: 15g, Fiber: 3g

91.Aussie Lamb Shanks with Red Wine Sauce

Prep Time: 15 mins
Cook Time: 2.5 hrs
Total Time: 2 hrs and 45 mins
Servings: 4

Ingredients:
- 4 lamb shanks
- Salt and pepper as needed
- 2 tbsp olive oil
- 1 onion, chop-up
- 2 carrots, diced
- 3 cloves garlic, chop-up
- 1 cup of red wine
- 2 cups of beef broth
- 1 can (14 oz) diced tomatoes
- 2 tbsp tomato paste
- 1 tsp dried rosemary
- 1 tsp dried thyme
- Fresh parsley for garnish

Instructions:
1. Set the oven temperature to 325°F (163°C).
2. Use salt and pepper to season the lamb shanks.
3. Heat the olive oil in a Big ovenproof pot over medium-high heat.
4. Shanks of lamb, brown on all sides. Take out and place aside.
5. Add the chop-up garlic, diced carrots, and chop-up onion to the same saucepan and sauté up to melted.
6. To deglaze the pot and scrape away any browned bits, pour in some red wine.
7. Add the diced tomatoes, tomato paste, dried thyme, and rosemary and stir.

8. Put the browned lamb shanks back into the pot and make sure the liquid covers them.
9. After bringing the mixture to a simmer, cover the pot and put it into the oven that has been preheated.
10. Bake the lamb shanks for two to three hrs, or up to they are soft and falling off the bone.
11. Before serving, garnish with fresh parsley.

Nutrition:
Cals: 400 per serving, Protein: 30g, Carbs: 10g
Fat: 25g, Fiber: 3g

92.Anzac Biscuit Energy Balls

Prep Time: 15 mins
Cook Time: 0 mins
Total Time: 15 mins
Servings: 12

Ingredients:
- 1 cup of rolled oats
- 1/2 cup of desiccated coconut
- 1/2 cup of almond butter
- 1/4 cup of honey
- 1/4 cup of golden syrup
- 1/2 tsp vanilla extract
- 1/4 cup of chop-up dried apricots
- 1/4 cup of chop-up walnuts
- Pinch of salt

Instructions:
1. Place rolled oats, almond butter, desiccated coconut, honey, golden syrup, vanilla extract, and a mini amount of salt in a mixer.
2. Pulse just up to the mixture forms a sticky dough and comes together.
3. After transferring the dough to a bowl, stir in the chop-up walnuts and dried apricots.
4. Form bite-sized balls by scooping out parts of the dough and rolling them.
5. Arrange the energy balls made of Anzac biscuits on a tray covered with parchment paper.
6. To firm up, refrigerate for a minimum of one hr.
7. Present and savour these energising Anzac biscuit nibbles!

Nutrition:
Cals: 150 per serving, Protein: 3g, Carbs: 15g
Fat: 8g, Fiber: 2g

93.Pumpkin and Macadamia Nut Soup

Prep Time: 15 mins
Cook Time: 30 mins

Total Time: 45 mins

Servings: 6

Ingredients:

- 1 medium-sized pumpkin, peel off, seeded, and diced
- 1 onion, chop-up
- 2 carrots, chop-up
- 3 cloves garlic, chop-up
- 1/2 cup of macadamia nuts
- 4 cups of vegetable broth
- 1 tsp ground cumin
- 1/2 tsp ground coriander
- Salt and pepper as needed
- 1/2 cup of coconut cream
- Fresh chives for garnish

Instructions:

1. Diced pumpkin, chop-up onion, chop-up carrots, chop-up garlic, and macadamia nuts Must all be mixd in a big pot.
2. Stir in the vegetable broth, salt, pepper, and ground cumin and coriander.
3. After bringing the mixture to a boil, lower the heat, and simmer the vegetables for 25 to 30 mins, or up to they are soft.
4. Puree the soup with an immersion blender up to it's smooth.
5. After adding the coconut cream, simmer for a further five mins.
6. Taste and adjust the seasoning.
7. Before serving, garnish with fresh chives.

Nutrition:

Cals: 250 per serving, Protein: 4g, Carbs: 20g

Fat: 18g, Fiber: 5g

94. Barramundi with Bush Tomato Pesto

Prep Time: 15 mins

Cook Time: 15 mins

Total Time: 30 mins

Servings: 4

Ingredients:

- For the Barramundi:
- 4 barramundi fillets
- Salt and pepper as needed
- 2 tbsp olive oil
- For the Bush Tomato Pesto:
- half a cup of drained sun-dried tomatoes in oil
- 1/4 cup of macadamia nuts
- 2 cloves garlic
- 1 cup of fresh basil leaves
- 1/2 cup of Parmesan cheese that has been finely grated

- 1/2 cup of olive oil
- Salt and pepper as needed

Instructions:

1. To prepare the barramundi, sprinkle some salt and pepper on the fillets.
2. In a skillet set over medium-high heat, warm the olive oil.
3. Barramundi fillets Must be seared for 3–4 mins on every side, or up to done.
4. For the Pesto de Bush Tomato:
5. Sun-dried tomatoes, macadamia nuts, garlic, basil, and Parmesan cheese Must all be mixd in a mixer.
6. Up to roughly chop-up, pulse.
7. Olive oil Must be added gradually while the processor is operating, up to the pesto has the consistency you want.
8. As needed, add salt and pepper for seasoning.
9. Arrange the barramundi fillets on plates for serving.
10. Drizzle with pesto made from bush tomatoes.
11. Savour the Barramundi with Pesto made from Bush tomatoes!

Nutrition (per serving):

Cals: 400, Protein: 30g, Carbs: 5g, Fat: 30g

Fiber: 2g

95. Vegemite and Cheese Toastie

Prep Time: 5 mins

Cook Time: 10 mins

Total Time: 15 mins

Servings: 2

Ingredients:

- 4 slices whole-grain bread
- Butter, melted
- Vegemite, as needed
- 1 cup of shredded cheddar cheese

Instructions:

1. Begin by preheating a pan or sandwich press.
2. Every bread piece Must have one side buttered.
3. On the side of two slices that isn't buttered, spread some Vegemite.
4. Put some shredded Cheddar cheese on top of the Vegetable Spread.
5. Place the remaining bread slices on top, buttered side out.
6. The cheese Must melt and the bread Must turn golden brown when the sandwiches are cooked.
7. Slice and present your Cheese Toast with Vegemite!

Nutrition (per serving):

Cals: 350, Protein: 15g, Carbs: 30g, Fat: 20g

Fiber: 5g

96. Salt and Pepper Crocodile Tacos

Prep Time: 20 mins
Marinating Time: 1 hr
Cook Time: 10 mins
Total Time: 1 hr 30 mins
Servings: 4

Ingredients:

- For the Crocodile:
- 1 lb crocodile meat, split into strips
- 1/4 cup of soy sauce
- 2 tbsp vegetable oil
- 1 tbsp sesame oil
- 1 tbsp honey
- 1 tsp black pepper
- 1 tsp garlic powder
- Other Taco Ingredients:
- 8 mini flour tortillas
- Shredded lettuce
- Split tomatoes
- Split avocado
- Sour cream
- Fresh cilantro, chop-up

Instructions:

1. To make the crocodile, mix the soy sauce, sesame oil, vegetable oil, honey, black pepper, and garlic powder in a bowl.
2. When the marinade is finished, add the crocodile strips and chill for at least an hr.
3. Crocodile strips Must be cooked through after two to three mins on every side in a skillet set over medium-high heat.
4. Regarding Taco Assembling:
5. Reheat the flour tortillas.
6. Place a few crocodile strips inside every tortilla.
7. Add split avocado, tomatoes, sour cream, chop-up cilantro, and shredded lettuce on top.
8. Serve your Crocodile Tacos with Salt & Pepper!

Nutrition (per serving):

Cals: 400, Protein: 25g, Carbs: 30g, Fat: 20g

Fiber: 5g

97. Tim Tam Ice Cream Sandwiches

Prep Time: 10 mins
Freezing Time: 2 hrs
Total Time: 2 hrs 10 mins
Servings: 4

Ingredients:

- 8 Tim Tam cookies
- 2 cups of vanilla ice cream
- Crushed Tim Tam for rolling

Instructions:

1. Place parchment paper into a baking dish.
2. Four Tim Tam cookies Must be placed in the dish's bottom.
3. Cover the cookies with a layer of vanilla ice cream.
4. Top with the final 4 Tim Tam cookies
5. Gently press to create a sandwich with the ice cream.
6. Freeze up to solid, or for at least two hrs.
7. Break up some more Tim Tam cookies and coat the ice cream sandwich edges with the crushed cookies.
8. Enjoy your Tim Tam Ice Cream Sandwiches after slicing them!

Nutrition (per serving):

Cals: 350, Protein: 4g, Carbs: 40g, Fat: 20g

Fiber: 1g

98. Bush Tomato Kangaroo Stew

Prep Time: 20 mins
Cook Time: 2 hrs
Total Time: 2 hrs 20 mins
Servings: 6

Ingredients:

- 1.5 lbs kangaroo stew meat, cubed
- 2 tbsp olive oil
- 1 onion, chop-up
- 3 cloves garlic, chop-up
- 2 carrots, split
- 2 potatoes, diced
- 1 cup of green beans, slice into 1-inch pieces
- 2 tbsp tomato paste
- 1 cup of red wine
- 4 cups of beef broth
- 1 tbsp bush tomato chutney
- 1 tsp dried thyme
- Salt and pepper as needed
- Fresh parsley for garnish

Instructions:

1. In a big pot, warm up the olive oil over medium-high heat.
2. When the kangaroo stew meat is added, brown it all over.
3. Add chop-up garlic and diced onion. Sauté the food up to it becomes tender.
4. Cook for two mins after adding the tomato paste.

5. After adding the red wine, scrape out any browned bits from the pot's bottom.
6. Add the dried thyme, dried tomatoes, green beans, carrots, potatoes, and beef broth.
7. After bringing to a boil, lower heat to a simmer, cover, and cook for two hrs, or up to meat is cooked.
8. Add fresh parsley as a garnish.
9. Serve Mashed Potatoes or Rice with your Bush Tomato Kangaroo Stew.

Nutrition (per serving):
Cals: 350, Protein: 30g, Carbs: 20g, Fat: 15g
Fiber: 5g

99.Aussie Lamb Shanks with Red Wine Sauce

Prep Time: 15 mins
Cook Time: 2.5 hrs
Total Time: 2 hrs 45 mins
Servings: 4

Ingredients:
- 4 lamb shanks
- Salt and pepper as needed
- 2 tbsp olive oil
- 1 onion, chop-up
- 3 cloves garlic, chop-up
- 2 carrots, split
- 2 celery stalks, chop-up
- 1 cup of red wine
- 2 cups of beef broth
- 2 tbsp tomato paste
- 2 tsp dried rosemary
- 2 tsp dried thyme
- Fresh parsley for garnish

Instructions:
1. Set the oven's temperature to 175°C/350°F.
2. Use salt and pepper to season the lamb shanks.
3. Heat the olive oil in a Big ovenproof pot over medium-high heat.
4. Shanks of lamb, brown on all sides.
5. Add the chop-up celery, split carrots, chop-up garlic, and diced onion. Toss the vegetables in a skillet and cook until they are soft.
6. Add tomato paste, red wine, beef broth, dried thyme, and rosemary.
7. Once it reverjes a simmer, cover the pot and put it inside the oven that has been warmed.
8. The lamb Must be baked for two to three hrs, or up to it is soft and falls off the bone.
9. Add fresh parsley as a garnish.

10. Serve your Red Wine Sauced Aussie Lamb Shanks over polenta or Mashed Potatoes.

Nutrition (per serving):
Cals: 450, Protein: 35g, Carbs: 15g, Fat: 25g
Fiber: 3g

100.Anzac Biscuit Energy Balls

Prep Time: 15 mins
Chilling Time: 1 hr
Total Time: 1 hr 15 mins
Servings: 12

Ingredients:
- 1 cup of rolled oats
- 1/2 cup of desiccated coconut
- 1/2 cup of almond meal
- 1/4 cup of chop-up macadamia nuts
- 1/4 cup of honey
- 1/4 cup of dilute coconut oil
- 1 tsp vanilla extract

Instructions:
1. Rolling oats, desiccated coconut, almond meal, chop-up macadamia nuts, honey, heated coconut oil, and vanilla essence Must all be mixd in a bowl.
2. Blend up to thoroughly blended.
3. The combination Must be chilled for at least an hr.
4. Roll the cooled mixture into bite-sized balls before rolling.
5. Arrange the Anzac Biscuit Energy Balls onto a parchment paper-lined tray.
6. Give it another fifteen mins to chill.
7. Savour your Energy Balls, Anzac Biscuits!

Nutrition (per serving - 2 balls):
Cals: 150, Protein: 2g, Carbs: 12g, Fat: 10g
Fiber: 2g

101.Pumpkin and Macadamia Nut Soup

Prep Time: 15 mins
Cook Time: 30 mins
Total Time: 45 mins
Servings: 6

Ingredients:
- 2 tbsp olive oil
- 1 onion, chop-up
- 3 cloves garlic, chop-up
- 1 mini pumpkin, peel off, seeded, and diced
- 1 Big potato, peel off and diced
- 1/2 cup of macadamia nuts

- 4 cups of vegetable broth
- 1 tsp ground cumin
- 1/2 tsp ground nutmeg
- Salt and pepper as needed
- 1 cup of coconut milk
- Fresh parsley for garnish

Instructions:

1. Warm up the olive oil in a big pot over medium heat.
2. Add chop-up garlic and diced onion. Sauté the food up to it becomes tender.
3. Add the diced macadamia nuts, diced pumpkin, and diced potato. Mix everything together.
4. After adding the veggie broth, bring it to a boil.
5. Vegetables Must be simmered for 20 to 25 mins, covered, or up to they are soft.
6. Puree the soup with an immersion blender up to it's smooth.
7. Add the ground nutmeg, cumin, and pepper and stir.
8. Stir in coconut milk and heat thoroughly.
9. Add fresh parsley as a garnish.
10. Warm up your Macadamia Nut and Pumpkin Soup.

Nutrition (per serving):

Cals: 300, Protein: 5g, Carbs: 25g, Fat: 20g

Fiber: 5g

102.Pepperberry Kangaroo Tacos

Prep Time: 15 mins
Cook Time: 10 mins
Total Time: 25 mins
Servings: 4

Ingredients:

- 1 lb kangaroo meat, thinly split
- 1 tbsp olive oil
- 1 tbsp ground pepperberry
- 1 tsp ground cumin
- 1 tsp smoked paprika
- Salt as needed
- 8 mini flour tortillas
- Shredded lettuce
- Diced tomatoes
- Split red onions
- Sour cream
- Fresh cilantro for garnish
- Lime wedges for serving

Instructions:

1. Split kangaroo meat Must be mixd with olive oil, smoked paprika, ground cumin, ground pepperberry, and salt in a bowl. Give it at least ten mins to marinate.
2. In a skillet, preheat the heat to medium-high.
3. Cook up to the marinated kangaroo meat is cooked to your preference, about 2 to 3 mins per side.
4. Use the skillet or microwave to reheat the tortillas.
5. Top every tortilla with a slice of kangaroo to assemble the tacos.
6. Add split red onions, diced tomatoes, shredded lettuce, and a dollop of sour cream on top.
7. Serve with lime wedges on the side and garnish with fresh cilantro.

Nutrition:

Cals: 300 per serving, Protein: 25g, Carbs: 25g, Fat: 10g, Fiber: 3g

Printed in Dunstable, United Kingdom